Lynda Thrift with Ivor Wood

Companion's Tales

Bumblebee Books

London

BUMBLEBEE PAPERBACK EDITION

Copyright © Lynda Thrift with Ivor Wood 2021

The right of Lynda Thrift with Ivor Wood to be identified as author of this work has been asserted in accordance with sections 77 and 78 of the Copyright, Designs and Patents Act 1988.

A CIP catalogue record for this title is available from the British Library.

ISBN: 978-1-83934-006-2

Bumblebee Books is an imprint of Olympia Publishers.

First Published in 2021

Bumblebee Books
Tallis House
2 Tallis Street
London
EC4Y 0AB

Printed in Great Britain

www.olympiapublishers.com

Dedication

For Daniel Kingsley Wood, and Victoria and Jessica

Acknowledgements

First and foremost, I would like to thank my good friend Ivor Wood. Without his inspiration and input, this book would not have happened. He provided the initial story outline and helped me to develop the plots.

I would also like to acknowledge the role played by Ivor's Labrador, Karen, as well as Fagan and Tilda on whom the main canine characters are based. And, of course, where would I be without my muse and companion in crime, Angela, better known as Mrs Pullalong?

As well as ideas and plots, there is a heap of work getting the stories down on paper. I would like to take this opportunity to thank my family and friends for their patience and understanding as this book came together. In particular, I would like to thank my wonderful cousins, Gordon and Pauline, for their proofreading skills!

It would be remiss of me to not thank Mariangela Grapps for her creative skills in bringing the book to life. Her watercolours have captured the storylines brilliantly.

I would also like to thank Gary Nickolls for his help and advice on layout so we could see how the illustrations fitted with the words. I think the end result speaks for itself. Thank you, Gary.

Finally, I would like to thank you for reading this book. I hope you enjoy it.

Other Titles in the Series

Contents

Chapter 1: Just Another Day

It was just another day.

Both Mrs Poser and Amble, her faithful Labrador, had finished their breakfasts, and it was time to start getting ready for their morning walk.

As Mrs Poser was pulling on her wellington boots, Amble skipped around her feet, and wished that she would hurry up. Didn't she realise that there were enticing smells outside just waiting to be sniffed? If she didn't hurry up, they might be lost for ever.

The two cats watched this scene from their vantage point on the top of the washing machine.

"It never changes, does it?" noted Teaser.

"You would think he would be bored!" agreed Wafter.

"I really don't understand it at all," continued Teaser. "I know that some smells — like roast chicken — are simply too good to ignore. But I really do not understand that creature's passion for sniffing trees and hedgerows. Unless there is a hint of mouse, I suppose!"

By now, Mrs Poser had finally completed her dog walking ensemble. She had her trusty waterproof coat and hat on 'because you just can't trust the weather', a roll of poo bags in her coat pocket 'because she was a responsible dog owner', and Amble's lead round her neck.

Her last task before opening the front door was to make sure that the cats had fresh water and food.

Wafter always came to investigate what morsels might be on offer. Teaser would often affect distain until Amble and Mrs Poser had left. Then he would rush over to the food bowl and make short work of his breakfast.

Today was just another day.

As Mrs Poser opened the door, and Amble rushed out, Teaser gave his full attention to the ball of wool which he had commandeered as his favourite toy. For today at least.

Amble gave a swift backward nod and bark to the cats then rushed through the door. He bumped straight into his best friend, Badger, the Border Collie.

As the two dogs sniffed their hellos, Mrs Pullalong came into view.

"Where shall we go today?" she asked.

The ladies decided that they should head towards the Wild Open Plains where the dogs could run and sniff and even swim to their hearts' delight — and the ladies wouldn't have to walk too far as they did so!

The ladies thought that this walk was an excellent start to the day. Their houses backed on to the Wild Open Plains, so the walk was easy to get to, and it meant that the ladies didn't get too tired at the start of the day. It also meant that the dogs would only have to walk on the lead for a short distance before being allowed to play.

So that was decided upon, and off they all went. It was such an ordinary day. Not too muddy, and not too wet. And it had been an excellent walk.

Amble was worn out and it wasn't even ten o'clock. Badger was thirsty and looking forward to a nice refreshing bowl of water.

The ladies had caught up on the gossip and they were now ready for a cup to tea.

And so they arrived back at the gate to Mrs Poser's house.

Badger was the first to notice.

"What's that in the hedge?" she asked Amble. "It looks like a ball of fur!"

Both the dogs had rushed over to investigate.

As they got closer, both dogs realised what — or rather who — it was.

Amble ran back to Mrs Poser straight away. This was not good at all, and so very important.

Mrs Poser heard Amble's bark and turned just as he stopped at her feet. Then she looked across to Badger and spotted the bundle in the hedge.

"Oh no!" she cried, running over. Mrs Pullalong followed.

Before Mrs Pullalong had moved two steps, Mrs Poser was already bending down and scooping up the small mass of fur. Then she let out a blood-curdling scream.

Mrs Pullalong immediately understood why.

The bundle of fur was Teaser — he was dead.

Mrs Pullalong pulled the two dogs away as Mrs Poser cradled her poor cat in her arms.

"He must have decided to cross the road and been hit by a car!" sobbed Mrs Poser.

The two dogs looked at each other in horror. Teaser was dead? This wasn't possible. When they had left to go on their walk, Teaser had been playing happily with a ball of wool. How could he be dead?

The troubled group, with Mrs Poser still cuddling Teaser, went into the house. Mrs Pullalong went to put the kettle on, but Mrs Poser said not to. Then she sat down; she was still holding Teaser and crying quietly.

And that was when the phone had started to ring.

Mrs Pullalong had answered, and as she did so, Amble said to Badger,

"This is horrible. I have never seen Mrs Poser like this before. What is going to happen?"

He stared at Mrs Poser's tear-stained face as Badger looked on.

Mrs Pullalong came back from the phone. Somewhere between putting the phone down and returning, she had found a large towel and a cup of tea.

"Here," she said as she handed the tea to Mrs Poser. "Drink this now. It's hot and sweet and it will help with the shock. Then we can put Teaser in this lovely warm fluffy towel. That was Mr Helpful on the phone. He is coming straight over!"

Mrs Poser took the tea but said nothing; she was still sobbing too hard to speak.

Chapter 2: Restless

On the other side of the Wild Open Plains, Adele, Amble's big sister, had felt restless since she had woken up. She had this funny feeling inside her. She could not settle. She paced up and down in front of Mr Helpful, who she lived with, and who was busy at his computer.

Mr Helpful looked up. He had just finished a long email to his sister, Harriet, who was selling her house in Scotland. She was moving to be closer to him and both he and Harriet were very much looking forward to it all happening.

He looked at Adele, watching as she prowled around. This wasn't at all like Adele. Mr Helpful wondered what the matter might be. It was not at all like her to be so fretful.

Mr Helpful encouraged her to go outside through the back door into the garden — perhaps a breath of fresh air would cheer her up? Mr Helpful watched anxiously through the kitchen window.

Adele wandered around, sniffing under the pergola where Mr Helpful had hung up seeds and peanuts to feed the birds. Although she paused, Adele did not eat up any of the fallen bird food.

"Oh dear, what can the matter be?" Mr Helpful thought to himself.

He knew that if a Labrador DIDN'T want to eat anything that was lying around, there must be something seriously wrong.

Mr Helpful watched as Adele slowly continued her walk around the garden. She took a listless look into the small pond to see if the goldfish were swimming around. Mr Helpful could see that she was doing this out of habit, not because she was interested in seeing her fishy friends. Then, she turned around, walked slowly back across the lawn and into the kitchen where she plopped herself into her basket.

There was no doubt about it. This dog was not happy.

Mr Helpful had an idea. He asked her, "Would you like a treat, Adele?"

On any other day, the promise of a treat would provoke much tail wagging. Indeed, it had never failed to get Adele's interest before. But today, Adele hardly moved. She didn't sit up, alert and eyes all aglow with expectation and excitement. She didn't do anything. She just sat there.

Mr Helpful by now was very concerned, even worried. What was troubling Adele so much?

He got down on his knees beside Adele, gently rubbed her ears and stroked her chin. On any other day, this was something that pleased and relaxed Adele.

"Tell me, Adele, what is THE matter? This is not like you at all. WHY are you so sad? Are you feeling poorly? Have you eaten something you shouldn't have eaten?"

Adele's eyes looked so sad, but she shook her head.

It wasn't any of those then, Mr Helpful concluded. It was all a bit of a mystery. What could he do to make things right?

As he pondered, Mr Helpful continued to kneel on the floor. Usually, if he did this for any length of time, his knees would start to ache and hurt. But not today. He was so lost in deep thought that he didn't notice.

He scratched his head. That didn't help one jot. He closed his eyes to see if that would help him think better, but that didn't work either.

What was he to do? He was so heavy-hearted. He didn't like Adele to be so sad.

Then Mr Helpful had another idea. He remembered Adele had not been to see her brother for quite a while. Perhaps a visit might cheer her up?

"Adele, would you like to go and see Amble? We haven't been for such a long time, and Mrs Poser is always so pleased to see us."

Adele looked up.

"Yes," she thought. "That might be the answer!"

She got up out of her basket and shook herself. Then, all the time, wagging her tail, she walked to the cupboard in the utility room where her lead was kept. Adele was all ready to go to see Amble that very second.

Mr Helpful was so relieved. He smiled that contented smile he had when he had solved a difficult problem.

But, before he did anything else, Mr Helpful decided to call Mrs Poser to make sure that she was in. There was no point at all driving over to see her if she wasn't there!

"Now, where did I leave that phone?" he muttered to himself. It was so much easier when phones were wired to the wall and you couldn't just put them down and then forget where you had left them. He wandered around the living room, searching.

Adele understood what was happening.

She knew that if he didn't find the phone, Mr Helpful wouldn't be able to call Mrs Poser. And then, they wouldn't be going anywhere. She wouldn't see Amble.

And then she would be back to feeling miserable.

As she watched Mr Helpful searching under cushions and the sofa for the elusive phone, she remembered where Mr Helpful had left it.

Quick as a flash, she ran into the study and returned with the phone in her mouth.

"Oh, Adele, you are such a clever girl! What would I do without you?" said Mr Helpful.

He grabbed the handset and tickled her ear as he continued,

"Typical Adele! You have come to my rescue! Let's call Mrs Poser right now!"

Chapter 3: Bad News

The phone rang and rang and rang, but just as Mr Helpful was about to put it down and abandon the idea of visiting, it was answered.

Strangely, though, it wasn't Mrs Poser that answered — it was Mrs Pullalong. Mrs Poser's neighbour and best friend who lived with Badger, Adele and Amble's best friend, and who didn't live at Mrs Poser's house. This was very odd.

"Oh, thank goodness it's you!" Mrs Pullalong said as she replied to Mr Helpful's, "Hello?"

She sounded very worried.

"What on earth has happened?" asked Mr Helpful. "Is Mrs Poser ill?"

"No, it's worse!" replied Mrs Pullalong.

"It's not Amble is it?" asked Mr Helpful. "He isn't ill?"

"No, it's not Amble, he's absolutely fine!"

Adele was listening to Mr Helpful talking. She noticed how his voice had changed from what she recognised as his 'telephone' voice to being very concerned. This was clearly very serious.

"Can you come over straightaway?" asked Mrs Pullalong. "I really think Mrs Poser would appreciate seeing you and Adele. It will take her mind off things, I think!

This sounded urgent. Mr Helpful didn't waste time to ask more. He would find out the details as soon as he got to Mrs Poser's house.

He grabbed Adele's lead, briefly checked to make sure he had poo bags, then put her in the back of the car and set off.

Truth be told, Mrs Poser was very, very sad and with good reason.

She had been out walking with Amble, Mrs Pullalong and Badger and then they had all come home to an absolute disaster.

What looked like a dirty ball of fur in the hedge by the garden had turned out to be Teaser. He was dead. So very dead.

Amble and Badger still couldn't believe it. Mrs Pullalong was shocked. Poor Mrs Poser was devastated.

None of them knew quite what to do.

Mrs Poser was sitting in her chair with poor dead Teaser curled up on her lap. She was distractedly sipping a cup of hot sweet tea as she stroked Teaser's ear. The dogs were sitting at her feet, wondering what they should do.

Then, Amble heard a car pull up outside. Badger heard it too. They both ran to the door to try to warn whoever it was to be careful. Teaser was dead, and Mrs Poser was sad and couldn't move from her chair.

Fortunately, Mrs Pullalong had also heard the car and had gone to the door to let the visitors in. As she did, the dogs rushed forward.

"Amble, what do you think you are doing? I nearly fell

over you!”

Amble knew that familiar, friendly voice. He was overjoyed. His tail wagged so fast and hard: it had never wagged so fast and hard before. His bark became so excited too. It was Mr Helpful, and Amble knew that where Mr Helpful was, Adele, his favourite sister, would be there too.

He hoped with every fibre of his being that they would be able to help. He really hoped that Adele could do something…

Oh, Adele!” Amble said. “Teaser has been knocked down and he’s dead. Mrs Poser is so upset. I am really worried about her.”

Adele gently nuzzled her head alongside Amble, and tenderly licked him.

“I could sense something wasn’t right!” Adele told Amble, “I didn’t know what, but there was something. That is why I persuaded Mr Helpful to drive over to see you and Mrs Poser. Mr Helpful will know what to do. Let us take him to find Mrs Poser.”

And that is precisely what Amble and Adele did.

Mrs Poser was slumped side-ways in her armchair, and still clutching Teaser, who was thankfully now wrapped in the towel. Adele thought that Mrs Poser looked a funny colour; her eyes were very red. But at least she had stopped crying.

Adele nudged Amble to tell him to follow him. Amble,

always happy to be with his big sister, wagged his tail to say that he would. Adele went out by the back door which was still open. The two Labradors trotted along together. Badger trailed behind. She wasn't quite sure what to do as nothing like this had ever happened to her before. And she certainly hoped that it wouldn't again. Ever.

"Where are we going, Adele?" Amble asked.

"We are going out of the way!" Adele said. "It's quite clear to me that Mrs Poser needs to think about what to do, and she won't be able to do that with us three dogs in the way!"

Back inside, Mrs Poser had started to recover from the shock, but she still didn't know quite what to do next.

However, she had noticed that the dogs had gone outside.

Mr Helpful pointed out that the dogs had realised that they needed to be out of the way.

Mrs Pullalong observed, "I saw Adele leading Amble and Badger outside. It would be just like her to notice that we needed to think. She came to our rescue and has given us the space to think!"

"Typical Adele — to the rescue again!" thought Mr Helpful to himself.

But now there were practicalities to be dealt with.

"Have you thought about where we might bury Teaser?" Mr Helpful gently asked.

Mrs Poser stifled another sob, as she realised that she couldn't keep on holding her poor dead cat for too much longer.

Mrs Pullalong looked out of the window, and towards the garden shed, where the cats had hidden not that long ago.

"There is a lovely little spot, just next to the shed where Teaser might like to be," she said. "It's warm and sunny so he won't feel the cold."

Mr Helpful offered to make a hole to bury Teaser in. Mrs Poser sadly, but gladly, agreed.

Mr Helpful helped the ladies prepare to say their last goodbyes to Teaser. The dogs were very subdued and were sniffing morosely around the garden.

Suddenly, Adele stopped. She had a horrible thought. More of a realisation, actually. No one had told Wafter that Teaser was dead. No-one had told Wafter that her best friend and partner in crime couldn't play out any more. Someone had to tell Wafter, and it was clear that Mrs Poser was in no fit state to do so.

It would be a terrible shock for Wafter, but she had to be told.

Adele went in search of the cat. It would be horrible news, and Adele wanted to break the news as gently as she could.

As luck would have it, Adele stumbled across Wafter who was asleep in the lavender bushes. She broke the news as kindly as she could.

Wafter's only response was, "So I am an only cat now?"

Which Adele thought was perhaps a little selfish, but then Wafter was a cat.

By now, Mr Helpful had completed his grim task, and the hole was deep and round. Mrs Poser stroked Teaser for the very last time then gently lowered him unto his resting place. Even Mrs Pullalong was crying now.

Mr Helpful said a short prayer, then everyone went back inside. The subdued dogs followed, vowing never to try to cross a road by themselves, EVER.

After Teaser had been buried, Mrs Pullalong and Mr Helpful made sure that Mrs Poser was going to be okay. At least she had stopped crying. There was little more that they could do there and then.

It was all so very sad. But for now, both Mr Helpful and Mrs Pullalong decided that all they could do was let Mrs Poser come to terms with what had happened by herself. They agreed that the right thing to do was to let Mrs Poser have a little time by herself.

Mr Helpful volunteered to take Amble for the rest of the day. Mrs Poser gladly agreed.

Mrs Pullalong and Badger went home, after telling Mrs Poser that they would call by and check up on her later.

But everyone was worried about what might happen in the coming days.

How would Mrs Poser cope without Teaser to help make her smile?

At the very least, there was now a yawning gap in her little family.

Chapter 4: Aftermath

It was a little cramped in the back of Mr Helpful's car, but Amble didn't mind snuggling up to his big sister. Indeed, given how awful it had been so far today, it was incredibly reassuring.

When they got back to Mr Helpful's house, both he and the two dogs didn't know quite what to do with themselves.

"Let's go for a walk!" suggested Mr Helpful. "It might take our minds off what has just happened."

And so, they did. It was a mark of how subdued Amble was that he didn't even tangle the leads as he and Adele walked side by side.

As Mr Helpful and the dogs walked down the street, Adele suddenly stopped. It was so sudden that Mr Helpful almost fell over her.

"What on earth is the matter this time?" he asked.

Adele whimpered and looked at the house she was outside. Mr Helpful looked in the same direction.

In the window of the house was a notice. It said, "Kittens: free to good home. Ready now!"

"You are such a clever girl!" Mr Helpful said as he patted Adele's head.

She might just have come to the rescue again! Here was a possible solution.

Mr Helpful knocked at the door and asked if he could view the kittens.

However, he left Adele and Amble tied to the lamp post outside as he didn't want to risk frightening the little ones.

When Mr Helpful saw the kittens, he could not believe his eyes. There were three little cats, each one with colouring very similar to that of Teaser.

He told the lady about Mrs Poser and asked if he could bring her to view the kittens. Of course, she said yes because she wanted them to find good homes.

Mr Helpful almost ran back home. He was so quick that both Adele and Amble were panting as they reached the door. But Mr Helpful didn't go in the house. Instead, he went to his car, opened the back door and told the dogs to get in. Then he put a box in the back as well. Now it was really cramped, and the dogs wondered what on earth was going on. They particularly wanted to know what the box for as it was really quite large!

Once he was satisfied that he had everything he needed, Mr Helpful drove back to Mrs Poser. Amble was a little disappointed — he had hardly had any time with his sister. But Mr Helpful didn't let the dogs out of the car. Instead, he rushed into Mrs Poser's house, and came out with her (still holding a crumpled tissue).

Then he drove straight back to the house where the kittens were.

Leaving a window open so that Adele and Amble didn't get too hot, he and Mrs Poser went into the house. After a few moments, Mr Helpful came out again and collected the mystery box. Amble thought this was quite odd. But Adele merely muttered, "Oh good. This is just as I had hoped!"

Then Mrs Poser who was now struggling to carry what was clearly now a quite heavy box, emerged. Mr Helpful stood at the door and shook the lady-of-the-house's hand. Mrs Poser struggled to carry the box, but she seemed a little more like her usual self. Amble thought that she was almost smiling.

"Let's go home!" she announced as she placed the box back next to the dogs.

When they got back, Mrs Poser almost leapt out of the car and ran inside, shouting, "I'll put the kettle on!" Meanwhile, Mr Helpful opened the back door of the car, retrieved the box and let the dogs out.

Amble was still confused but Adele seemed to know what had happened.

"Just wait and see!" she advised as the dogs followed Mr helpful inside.

Wafter, who had been watching the birds in the garden, also decided to follow. She was curious to find out what all this to do was about. She was a cat after all — and an only cat at that!

Amble came through the door; Wafter followed at a safe distance. She wanted to know what was going on but didn't want to risk being picked up. She simply wasn't in the mood and as an only cat she felt that it was only right that her wishes should be honoured.

As the animals came into the kitchen, they saw Mr Helpful pouring a pot of tea. Then, when everyone was settled, Mrs Poser opened the box.

Out tumbled not one, not two, but THREE little ginger kittens. Each looking quite a lot like Teaser.

So that was what the box was for! To carry these tiny mites.

Mrs Poser looked at Amble's surprised face and chuckled.

"Amble, meet Eany, Meany and Mo. They are coming to live with us! I couldn't decide which one of these delightful creatures would cheer me up the most, so I decided to have all three!"

Amble sniffed each kitten in turn and introduced himself. Adele looked on with a happy smile. Wafter looked appalled. She had been quite looking forward to being an only cat. Mrs Poser called to Adele and gave her a special treat.

"This is to say thank you for all your help today. You have come to my rescue not once, but three times!"

Mr Helpful was also smiling. He was so proud of Adele.

She had realised that there was something wrong and got him to visit Mrs Poser. She had kept the dogs out of the way while the humans decided what to do.

And, perhaps most importantly, she had found the kittens who were going to make sure that Mrs Poser was going to be all right.

Not to mention knowing where Mr Helpful had left the phone!

Typical Adele! What a star.

Chapter 5: Settling In

Eany, Meany and Mo were in a state of shock. What had just happened?

Only a short time ago, they had been curled up next to each other under the watchful eye of their mother.

They all knew that this time would come. Mummy had warned them about it. She had told them many times that they were now old enough to go out into the world on their own. She hoped that they would be adopted by a loving family that didn't have children who wanted to chase them and chew their tails.

The kittens also hoped that they would go to good homes. However, they knew that, once they went to their new homes, they would probably never see their mummy, or even each other, ever again.

So, the kittens were prepared for that day. But not for it to happen just yet.

It was just lovely to snooze wrapped around each other with their heads resting on their mummy's tummy. It was so peaceful to lie there and listen to her purr and tell them how much she loved them and she was so proud of them. That she was sure that they would all have long happy lives.

And then, a strange man and even stranger woman had come with a box and put them into it. Then there was a lot of jolting around, until now.

They had been unceremoniously tipped from the box, and now there they were on a rug in front of a table.

They looked around with frightened scared eyes.

They could see the strange lady and the man, and another lady looking back at them. Next to them were three dogs: two looking almost identical (although it had to be admitted that one was a little tubbier than the other) and a slightly smaller black and white dog, which, truth to tell, seemed to be quite nervous of them!

It was very peculiar and not at all what or how the kittens thought the next stage of their life would be.

They had fondly imagined that they would be told a few days before they were due to leave that new homes had been found for them. They had expected some time to say their goodbyes to each other and Mummy. But that hadn't happened at all; it had been quick, sharp, and possibly even brutal. One minute they were with Mummy, and the next they were in a place that had not a sliver of her scent.

They were very, very frightened.

"Come along," said the strange lady who had carried them in the box. "Let's leave the kits to explore and settle in. It must be all a little scary for them right now! We can introduce ourselves later."

"Good idea," agreed the man.

"Anyone for a cup of tea?" asked the other lady.

Then they walked out of the room, and, much to the kittens' relief, the dogs followed them.

"I don't like this!" exclaimed Eany.

"I want my mummy!" meowed Meany.

Mo simply felt incredibly sad.

As the kittens morosely sniffed their way around the furniture, they became aware of another presence. One that had a vaguely familiar smell, but not really.

Another cat. Another cat who was completely grown up and who obviously lived here too.

"Hello, children."

The kittens looked up and there, in front of them, was Wafter.

"I suppose you have come to live here," Wafter continued.

"It's only fair to tell you now that I am Top Cat here. I was going to be an only cat until you turned up, and I can see that you are here to stay. Just be aware that I am the Top Cat now and will be for ever. None of you can ever take my place.

There are a number of rules that you must obey if we are to get along. If you don't, then Mrs Poser may not feed you, and she may even give you away!"

The kittens were now really frightened. What sort of place had they been brought to? And who was this 'Mrs Poser' person? She sounded quite fearsome.

Little did the kittens realise that Wafter was really just as nervous of them as they were of her.

Wafter knew she had to make it clear that she was the boss now or they would try to take over.

But if she set some rules now, she might be Top Cat for a while at least.

Wafter started to wash herself in that sinister way that cats do.

As she lazily licked her paws, she continued to lecture the kittens.

"The most important rule is, of course, to remember that I am Top Cat. What I say goes. It is the law. You must do as I say all the time. Otherwise, I will tell Mrs

Poser and then she might get rid of you!"

The kittens huddled together. Not only were they in a strange place, this cat was more than a little intimidating.

"Rule two — you must NEVER go out onto the road! My very good friend, Teaser, was killed as he tried to cross the road outside. He forgot to look both ways before leaving the pavement. A car came along and hit him. He died!"

This was stark news.

Wafter continued.

"So, you must never, ever, ever try to cross the road outside. I don't want Mrs Poser to get upset again like she was with Teaser."

Then, almost to herself, Wafter added, "But of course, if you did decide to get yourself killed, I would become an only cat again, which would be very nice!"

The kittens were both in awe and afraid of Wafter. She was almost like a school teacher as she continued to set out what the kittens should and should not do.

And by the time she had finished, their poor little heads were buzzing with so much information.

They decided that they needed to hide away and sit down so they could absorb it all. After all, they were new here, and they didn't want to make any mistakes.

This was their home now, and they had to make it work.

They may have a bossy cat in charge of them, and dogs and odd humans, but they couldn't go home. For the very simple reason that they didn't have a clue how to get there.

As they hid behind the curtain, the kittens heard voices in the distance, and then a door slamming. Then the noise of a car engine starting.

"Well," said Eany. "This is it. The first day of the rest of our lives!"

"I'm not sure I like it!" said Meany.

"I'm not sure we have a choice," observed Mo.

Just as he said this, Mrs Poser came back into the room. She didn't try to find the kittens as she knew they would be trying to adjust to being with her. Instead, she put down some bowls of special kitten food, some water and a litter tray.

Then she told Wafter to leave, and gently closed the door.

The kittens poked their pink noses out from under the curtain.

"It's all quiet again," said Meany. "Do you think it's safe to come out?"

Mo had already decided it was and had started to tuck into the food.

"Hey, you two," he shouted. "Come over here and try this. It's delicious. If you don't come and join me I am going to eat it all!"

When Eany and Mo saw how brave Mo was, they decided to follow his example. And he was right. The food was delicious.

After they had eaten their fill and done what they needed to in the litter tray, they all climbed onto the sofa and snuggled up to a cushion. It wasn't their mother, but it was almost as comfortable, and they were so very tired. It had been a very stressful day and they were only little. So, of course, they fell fast asleep.

Chapter 6: New Friends

As dawn broke, the kittens woke up with a jolt. They had completely forgotten where they were.

It was all still so very new and they didn't really understand what was happening at all.

As they rubbed their eyes, they could see that the door was opening again, and the lady was coming in with more bowls of food and one of the dogs from yesterday. The ever so slightly tubby one. The one that had sniffed them all over. Eany had a vague memory that the dog had told them his name, but the kitten had been so frightened that he hadn't remembered it at all.

"Hello, Boys," the lady said in the gentle voice that they recognised from the day before. "I hope you had a good sleep. I know this is all very strange for you, but I thought you should meet us all properly now. You met Wafter yesterday, but I didn't have a chance to introduce you to myself or the other member of our household. I am Mrs Poser, and I am going to look after you from now on."

So this was the fearsome Mrs Poser that Wafter had warned them about.

She didn't look scary at all. A bit odd, in her tatty jeans and fleece, but definitely not scary.

The kittens looked at each other and wondered if they had understood Wafter properly.

Mrs Poser turned to the dog, who had followed her in. He looked calm and gentle and, as yesterday, still ever so slightly tubby.

He sat down and offered the kittens his paw.

Mrs Poser continued her introductions.

"This is Amble. He is my companion and looks after me when I go out for walks. I am sure if you ask him nicely, he will be your friend too."

The kittens nervously walked towards Amble. Their mother had warned them about dogs. She said that they were ferocious and wild. That they would chase them up trees, and bite their tails (a bit like children, who she had also warned against.)

But this dog had kind amber-coloured eyes, and he was offering them his paw.

"Hello," he said. "I remember coming here when I was little, and I was so scared and frightened. But I learnt very quickly that Mrs Poser is the kindest person in the whole world — except for Mrs Pullalong, who of course doesn't

live here — and she will look after you and make sure that you are happy.

I suppose Wafter has already laid down the law. But don't worry too much about that. If you think about it, there are three of you, and only one of her, so she needs to make sure you know your place!"

With this, the kittens were reassured. Here was a friendly face at last. It was just what they needed. Someone who understood how they felt and knew what it felt like to be in a new home.

Mrs Poser looked on happily as the kittens moved closer to Amble and sniffed his face. Then Amble tried to lick them. It so reminded Mrs Poser of the licking competitions that he and Teaser had had in what already felt to be a lifetime ago.

It was a lovely scene.

"I think you probably remember Mr Helpful and Mrs Pullalong from when you arrived. And you might also remember Adele and Badger."

So that explained who was on the welcoming committee when they had first arrived. They were friendly. The kittens weren't too sure who was who or what yet, but at least they had names to work with now.

But Mrs Poser hadn't finished yet.

"I do have two more important people that I want you to meet soon. But perhaps not just yet. I want you to settle in properly. But you will meet them soon. They are my grandchildren! When they next visit, I will introduce you to them properly."

As she said this, she put down the fresh food, and Wafter came in through the open door behind her.

"So, she has told you about her grandchildren. Don't be fooled. They are a threat to catdom. I know them well!

That Baby is growing up and learning to be gentle. Although she does still want to rub her face in your fur — well, she does to me anyway — which isn't particularly pleasant. But That Other Baby is a real menace. All he wants to do is chase you and chew your tail! Be warned — you need to be on your guard. You can't scratch them, or you will be in SERIOUS TROUBLE. The best thing you can do when they come is to HIDE!"

For once, Wafter had shared some wise words. The kittens recognised this and decided to remember them well. Perhaps Wafter wasn't as fearsome as she seemed.

Having said her piece, Wafter followed Amble and Mrs Poser out of the room, and Mrs Poser quietly closed the door.

When they were alone again, Meany said, "There seems to be an awful lot that we need to remember!"

The others agreed.

"But Mrs Poser seems nice and the dog is very friendly. And he lives here, and his friends don't. I will reserve judgment and keep out of the way of his friends," said Mo.

Again, wise words.

And with that, the kittens started to explore the room again. They knew they had a lot to learn but were starting to feel a little more at home — at least in this room. What may or may not be outside of it was for another day.

Chapter 7: Surprise

Mrs Poser and Mrs Pullalong were enjoying a cup of tea as the two dogs sat outside in the garden.

The dogs were bored and couldn't understand how a cup of tea could be more interesting than throwing a ball for them. It was a gloriously sunny day — the sort that doesn't happen too often. The ladies were wasting it drinking warm brown liquid. No, Amble and Badger couldn't understand it at all.

However, it was how it was and all they could do was wait. Something would happen soon.

Mrs Poser and Mrs Pullalong were discussing the kittens, and particularly how well they had started to settle in.

It was still early days, but Mrs Poser had now allowed the little ones into the whole house and was thinking of letting them start to explore the garden soon.

She told Mrs Pullalong how the kittens made her smile with their antics. One of them — Mo apparently, although Mrs Poser couldn't be too sure as she was still having difficulty telling them apart — had even fallen asleep in Amble's food bowl.

Mrs Pullalong observed that that sleeping in a dog bowl wasn't perhaps the most sensible bed a little cat could have chosen, but it did show that the kittens trusted Amble.

As the ladies chatted, the dogs heard a car pulling up next to the house. Then, as they readied themselves to bark at whoever it was, Adele came bounding around the corner. This was an unexpected pleasure for both Amble and Badger — not to mention a welcome distraction from having to wait for the ladies to finish their tea.

Amble and Badger immediately invited Adele to join them in a game of chase, and Adele accepted joyfully. The dogs started to run and jump over the lawn, through the lavender bushes and under the shrubs, and generally have a good time.

Meanwhile, inside the kitchen, Mrs Poser had put the kettle on again and was making another cup of tea. Mr Helpful pulled up a chair to join them.

"This is a bit of a surprise," said Mrs Poser as she put a small amount of milk into the cup. "To what do we owe the pleasure?"

"Not that we aren't delighted to see you," added Mrs Pullalong, hastily.

"I do have some news that I would like to share," said Mr Helpful. "It's something totally unexpected and has only just happened. I wanted to share it with you straight away! And I also wanted to find out how your new friends are setting in!"

Mrs Poser smiled at this last comment. She had already fallen head over heels in love with her three new ginger kittens and was only too happy to share this fact.

She was pleased to report that Amble had accepted them right away and was even letting them chase his tail!

Wafter had been a little more reticent, but was starting to realise that if she could bring herself to tolerate them, she was rewarded with her favourite food.

Mr Helpful was so pleased to hear that all was going well. He could see that Mrs Poser was back to her usual self, which was a huge relief. Both he and Mrs Pullalong had been so worried about her when Teaser had been killed.

Thank goodness Adele had spotted the notice advertising the kittens and thank goodness she had been able to draw it to Mr Helpful's attention.

Without that, it was highly likely that Mrs Poser would still be distraught and upset about Teaser. But now, although she was still clearly sad about what had happened, the three kittens were able to distract her and make her smile.

After asking about the kittens, Mr Helpful settled down with his tea and told the ladies his news.

It seemed that he had bought some raffle tickets when he was in the local shop. The money raised from the raffle was going to be donated to a local charity (towards repairing the village hall roof, he thought, which was a good cause). The top prize was for a real live chef to come to the winner's home and cook a five-course (yes — five-courses!) meal for the winner and up to seven more guests. Wouldn't that be lovely? A posh meal, all cooked for you, and served to you, just like in a restaurant or café — but in your own home?

Mrs Pullalong and Mrs Poser agreed — no washing up either!

Now came the exciting bit.

It seemed that the raffle had taken place a few days ago. Mr Helpful had just received a letter from the organisers that very morning to tell him that he had won the top prize! It was he who was going to have the chef come to his home and cook a five-course meal!

Both the ladies were amazed. For a start, they had never actually met anyone who had won anything in a raffle before. And certainly, never anyone who had won such a fabulous prize! Gosh!

Tea was forgotten as both Mrs Poser and Mrs Pullalong demanded to know more. When was the meal? What food would he have? And perhaps most importantly — who was Mr Helpful going to invite to join him?

"Of course, I want you both to come!" said Mr Helpful. "You are my best friends and it wouldn't be right if you weren't able to come. And I want you to bring the dogs as well. I have told the chef about them and he doesn't mind!"

"Harriet is also going to come, and so is Gentleman Jim. It will be a huge party for all the people who are dear to me!"

It all sounded lovely! So lovely, in fact, that they decided to take the dogs out for a walk so that they could talk about it all while enjoying the sunshine.

They called to the dogs as they prepared for the walk.

Sensible shoes — check!

Poo bags — check!

Leads — check!

And, lastly, dogs — check!

The happy group went through the back gate and out on to the Wild Open Plains.

The dogs were delighted. As they ran around, Adele brought Amble and Badger up-to-date with Mr Helpful's news and plans.

Badger was amazed. Mrs Pullalong often cooked mince and carrots for her. But that was only one course of food, and at this chef meal, there would be four more as well!

Badger couldn't imagine five whole courses all at the same time. It would surely be too much food, and then she wouldn't be able to run around.

However, both Amble and Adele could imagine five lots of dinner all at the same time. Indeed, it would be a dream come true for a Labrador. As Labradors, Amble and Adele both thought the idea of a five-course meal sounded marvellous!

Then Amble shivered.

"I remember watching a cooking show on television when I had my cut paw and couldn't walk," he said. "The chef wore a white hat and a white coat!"

The other two dogs stopped running to listen.

Amble reminded them of how, when he was going to be a guide dog, he had messed up his test by running into a butcher's shop, and if that wasn't bad enough, he had then been chased out of the butcher's shop by a man wearing a white coat.

"Since that awful day, "Amble continued. "I have been afraid of men in white coats! What shall I do?"

Adele and Badger looked

at each other. They knew Amble was afraid of men in white coats. And they also knew that Amble was right that chefs wore white coats. Oh dear. Would this mean that he wouldn't be able to come to the posh dinner with them?

Coincidentally, Mrs Poser was asking the same question of Mr Helpful.

She particularly remembered how Amble had frozen with fear when she had tried to walk with him past the local butcher's shop. And then how, when the butcher had come outside to see what was happening, Amble had growled at him.

She had been so relieved that Amble had been safely on his lead and quite a distance away, but it was still not a pleasant experience for either her or Amble. Fortunately, the butcher had been very understanding and had even given Amble a sausage to try to show that he was a nice man. But Mrs Poser had never taken Amble past anyone wearing a white coat since, just in case.

As ever, though, Mr Helpful had remembered Mrs Poser telling him the story. And, because he was such an organised person, he had already talked about Amble with the chef. After all, Mr Helpful didn't want to frighten the chef!

Apparently, it was all sorted. While it is true that chefs usually wear white coats and hats, they can also wear striped aprons, which cover up most of the white coat. Chef had agreed to do this.

Although a stripy apron would cover up most of a white coat, Mrs Poser was still concerned. Then she had an idea.

Mrs Poser said "I have a stripy apron! Do you think your chef would let me borrow one of his white coats? I will wear it and the apron whenever I am in the kitchen. That way, Amble will get used to seeing what your chef will be wearing on the night, and stop being afraid!"

Mr Helpful thought this was a splendid idea. Mrs Pullalong was less certain but thought it was probably worth trying. And she also wanted to see Mrs Poser dressed like a chef. It would make such a change from the more usual dog walking clothes!

So that was decided upon.

And with that decision came another, which was for Mrs Poser, Mrs Pullalong and Mr Helpful to go back to Mrs Poser's house for another cup of tea.

Chapter 8: Facing Fears

Amble rushed downstairs for his breakfast. He had slept particularly well after playing out with Badger and Adele.

He barked to let Mrs Poser know he was on his way as he entered the kitchen. And then he stopped. There, in front of him, was a white-coat-clad Mrs Poser, complete with stripy apron and chef's hat. She was holding a bowl of his favourite dog food.

Amble didn't know what to do. Here was the embodiment of all his worst fears. In his kitchen and being worn by the person he loved most in the whole world. And she was holding a bowl of his favourite dog food.

He was confused. Very confused. He knew he should be scared. But this was Mrs Poser, with a bowl of his favourite food. What should he do?

To be fair, as a Labrador, it didn't take him long to decide. Given that food was involved, Amble rapidly decided he wasn't really afraid. Indeed, he would offer Mrs Poser his paw, and he would be rewarded with his favourite food.

But he hoped she wouldn't do this to him again.

He might not be afraid of it now but she was wearing it. He knew full well that if anyone else had been wearing it, he would have been absolutely terrified.

And to be fair, although Amble wasn't scared, he knew in his heart of hearts that he was still quite nervous of the white coat - even though it was Mrs Poser wearing it.

Amble certainly didn't want Mrs Poser to make any sudden moves that might startle him. She might not realise it, but if she made him jump, he might forget all his training and bite her!

Amble decided to concentrate on his food instead and push the dark thoughts to the back of his mind.

Fortunately, after breakfast, Mrs Poser changed into her dog walking clothes. Amble breathed a sigh of relief. Now he could put the awful episode behind him.

The intrepid duo set off briskly for a lovely long walk across the Wild Open Plains, into Mystery Wood and then round the plains again. They got back just in time for lunch.

As Amble busied himself with making sure that everything was where he had left it, Mrs Poser changed back out of her dog walking clothes. Then she called to him.

As he turned around, he got the shock of his life.

Yes, it was Mrs Poser.

But she was wearing the scary chef's whites again — complete with tall hat and stripy apron.

Amble ran and hid behind the sofa. He was terrified. He thought all this strange behaviour was over. Hadn't they just enjoyed a lovely walk together? What was Mrs Poser doing to him?

First, she was nasty wearing white, then she was nice with lovely food and a good walk, and now she was back to being nasty again.

As he quivered behind the sofa, Mrs Poser came and knelt next to it.

"Do come on out, Amble," she pleaded. "It's only me. I am trying to get you used to white coats and chefs' hats before we go to Mr Helpful's posh dinner. If you can't get used to them, and stop being quite so afraid of white coats, I might not be able to take you. And I am not missing out on a five-course meal because you are afraid of men in white coats. If you can't get over this, I will have to leave you at home!"

Amble didn't know what to do. He had been afraid of men in white coats ever since that awful day when he had been chased out of the butcher's shop when he was a puppy.

Then he started to think. Perhaps he was being a little too sensitive? After all, he hadn't been chased by a man in white coat since that day.

And to be fair, although the cricket teams wore white shirts and trousers, he wasn't afraid of them. In fact, he loved them. They always gave him sandwiches to eat if he happened to walk past the pavilion when they were having tea.

And he certainly shouldn't be afraid of white coats when Mrs Poser was wearing them.

No, it was time to be brave and face up to his fear. He had suffered long enough, especially if it meant that he wouldn't be able to go to the posh meal if he didn't get his act together.

Amble timidly poked his nose out from behind the sofa. Mrs Poser was still kneeling there. Still in her chef's whites.

"Come on, Amble," she coaxed in a gentle voice. "Let's try to overcome your fear together. Remember how Sammy used to be afraid of you? But simply by being around you, over time, he got to realise that you weren't frightening. And now, he even takes you for walks!"

Amble did indeed remember. He couldn't understand why the little boy up the road had been so scared of him. After all, Amble was a Labrador, a dog renowned for being gentle, placid and kind. There was nothing to be afraid of. Not of him anyway.

And, yes, it had taken some time, but little by little, Sammy had grown in confidence as he had become used to Amble being around and realised that nothing bad had happened.

Amble snuffled up to Mrs Poser and licked her hand.

"There we go, my brave boy!" Mrs Poser said. "I don't expect that you will get your confidence overnight. We are going to work on this, and by the time we go to Mr Helpful's, you won't be worried by men in white coats at all."

Amble gritted his teeth.

"I have to do this! And I will do this!" he muttered to himself.

Mrs Poser continued. "From now on until we go to Mr Helpful's posh

meal, I will wear the white coat and hat so that you can get used to seeing them. And then, hopefully when you see the chef, you won't mind at all!"

Amble managed a small smile to himself. He knew why Mrs Poser was doing this. He really did want to stop being afraid of white coats and he had to admit that Mrs Poser did look ridiculous in a white coat and chef's hat.

What on earth would Badger and Mrs Pullalong say when they came around?

Amble realised that he was hoping that he and Badger would have a good laugh about it all.

With that thought, Amble also realised that it was highly likely that Mrs Poser's strange behaviour was starting to work already.

After all, until a few minutes ago, he had been hiding behind the sofa. And now, he was thinking about having a laugh with Badger at how funny Mrs Poser looked dressed in chef's whites.

Amble continued to muse that although he would never want to go in or even near a butcher's shop ever again, regardless of what tactics Mrs Poser might try. However, there was a very good chance that he could overcome his fear of men in white coats.

At least until after the posh five-course meal, at least.

But they would never be his favourite thing!

Chapter 9: Fine Dining

The day had finally arrived.

Amble watched with amusement as Mrs Poser got herself ready for Mr Helpful's posh meal.

At last the chef's whites had been put to one side.

Now Mrs Poser was trying to fasten up her best dress. It was one that she had had for a little while and that she had just collected from the dry cleaners.

As Mrs Poser struggled to force the zip up, she muttered, "It must have shrunk at the cleaner's!"

Amble smiled to himself. He knew full well that it hadn't shrunk at all — it was Mrs Poser's passion for ginger biscuits which was causing her current problems.

Eventually, though, the zip was forced to close (nipping a little of Mrs Poser's skin in the process). Mrs Poser smoothed the fabric down and sighed (but not too hard — the dress was still quite tight), looked at herself in the mirror and decided that she would do. Just so long as she didn't eat too much or try to bend over!

The last time Amble had seen her take so much trouble to get ready was when they were at the seaside.

Amble remembered how he had seen her carefully select a dress (rather than the jeans that she usually wore) and shoes with heels.

He hadn't realised then that all this dressing up had meant that she was going to go out and leave him. He shuddered as he remembered how he had been left in the car while Mrs Poser went to eat, and how he had watched the stars come out. He also remembered very strongly that he hadn't liked it one little bit.

However, that was then and this was now.

Amble looked across to the bed where the chef's whites lay rumpled on the bedspread. He knew that he wasn't going to be left outside in a car in the dark this time. This time, he was going to be with Mrs Poser, Mrs Pullalong and Badger at Mr Helpful's house. Where they were going to enjoy a huge five-course luxury meal, cooked by a professional chef no less!

Amble would be deeply offended if that didn't happen —
especially after all his and Mrs Poser's preparations! He had
watched Mrs Poser wear those awful chef's whites for what
felt like days now and, partly to please her (but mainly so he
could join in the five-course meal), he had tried hard to not be
afraid of them. And Amble was almost sure that all their hard
work had paid off. But, of course, both he and Mrs Poser knew
that they would only find out just how successful they had
been when they got to Mr Helpful's house.

There was a knock at Mrs Poser's door. Mrs Poser opened
it and there was a rather glamorous Mrs Pullalong standing on
the doorstep.

"I hope you are both ready!" she said as Amble rushed out
to find Badger.

But Badger wasn't there.

"I had terrible trouble finding a taxi that would take
both us and the dogs to Mr Helpful's house," Mrs Pullalong
continued as Amble continued to search for his friend. Had
Mrs Pullalong had to leave her behind?

"But eventually, I found one that takes both dogs and
people, and its HUGE!"

As she said this, Amble
heard a joyful bark from the
car which was parked by the
gate. Badger was already in
the taxi! What a relief!

Amble rushed to the
car door and barked to Mrs
Poser to hurry up. They
were all ready to go for a
five-course meal, and he

didn't want to miss a single course.

Mrs Poser got into the taxi very carefully. Mrs Pullalong thought it was because Mrs Poser didn't want to crease her dress, which did, it had to be admitted, look very smart, if just a tiny bit tight. Amble knew the real reason why Mrs Poser was being so careful though. It was precisely because the dress was a tiny bit tight!

When everyone was settled with seat belts and dog restraints secured, they set off.

Before you could say, 'are we nearly there?', they had arrived.

Mrs Pullalong was first out of the taxi. She went to the front door and knocked loudly.

The dogs and Mrs Poser followed behind.

Harriet, Mr Helpful's sister, opened the door and let everyone in.

Amble rushed over to Adele.

"Where is the chef?" he asked.

He needed to know if the chef was dressed in white.

Adele licked her brother and calmly told him, "The chef is in the kitchen and he is very busy, which is why we aren't allowed in there. But even if we were, you have nothing to fear. Chef knows that you are scared of men in white coats and so he has decided to wear his chequered uniform instead. So, there are no white coats and no tall hats to be afraid of at all. Isn't that wonderful?"

Amble felt like a huge weight had been lifted from his shoulders. Even though he thought he was ready to face a chef in a white coat, it was good to know that he wasn't going to be put to the test. Now he could relax and enjoy himself properly.

Badger agreed. She said, "That's a relief! Not that it would have put you off your food, Amble! But you might have had a dose of indigestion!"

Meanwhile, Mr Helpful had settled the ladies on the comfortable settee and was offering them a glass of sherry each (as it was a special occasion). Harriet busied herself putting their coats away.

Then there was a loud noise, and everyone jumped. They looked across to where the noise had come from. There was Chef, standing in the doorway to the dining room. He was holding a small gong in his hand.

"Now I have your attention," he announced. "Dinner is served!"

And so, the culinary adventure began.

Mrs Poser was so hungry. She hadn't eaten all day, so she would have enough room in her tummy to enjoy five-courses.

As the first course arrived (fresh asparagus with butter), Mrs Poser looked at the portion size. It looked quite small.

Mrs Poser thought that she would still be hungry after the meal was finished at this rate. (Which, considering how tight her dress was, probably wasn't a bad thing!)

Although there wasn't a lot of it, the asparagus was absolutely delicious.

Meanwhile, the dogs tucked into their first course which was a small portion of Badger's favourite mince and carrots.

After a polite pause, the empty plates were cleared away and the next course was served.

This time it was a tomato soup. Mrs Pullalong was concerned that it might be cold by the time she got hers as she was at the end of the table, and when she tasted it, she was right: it was cold.

But as she wondered whether she should say something, chef announced, "This soup is called gazpacho. It is Spanish, and it is meant to be served cold. Don't worry. Just try it!"

Well, have you ever heard the like? Cold soup! This was going to be an adventure!

What else was going to be on the menu?

Meanwhile, the dogs had been served their second course — a light chicken broth with tiny pieces of chicken. The dogs thought it was wonderful. Just not enough of it!

And so, the meal progressed. During the fish course (a small slightly spicy fishcake with an unusual sauce), Mr Helpful and Harriet talked about Harriet's move from Scotland. Mrs Poser asked if she had settled in her new place, and when the ladies might visit!

Mrs Pullalong wanted to know whether Harriet would now be able to have a cat.

It somehow seemed appropriate to talk about cats while eating a fish course.

As course number four approached, Mrs Poser realised that she was starting to feel quite full.

Nevertheless, the roast lamb with all the trimmings (and especially those crispy roast potatoes) smelt too good to miss. She would just have to force herself!

The dogs, too, were enjoying their roast lamb. But they weren't feeling full at all.

Adele gave a discrete burb. Badger licked her lips with pleasure.

"I could get to like this sort of meal!" said Badger.

Amble was too busy wondering what the next plate of delights would be to comment.

Finally, it came to pudding.

Before it was brought out of the kitchen, Mr Helpful called for a pause in proceedings. He wanted to make a short speech, and particularly to thank the chef for all his splendid work.

"And now," Mr Helpful, concluded. "We come to our final course. We were all both bemused and inspired by Mrs Poser's and Amble's foray into the Antipodes…"

"Where's that?" interrupted Mrs Pullalong.

"I think he's referring to Mrs Poser's trip to Australia,"

whispered Harriet.

Mr Helpful didn't hear these asides and so continued without pausing for breath.

"And so, our last course is to help us celebrate Mrs Poser's time away and her most welcome return home!"

Without seeming to move an inch, he dimmed the lights as chef brought out a fluffy white meringue filled with strawberries and cream and lit by three bright sparklers.

"It's a pavlova!" gasped Mrs Poser, whose eyes were shimmering as she remembered how torn she felt between living at home and being in Australia.

Amble looked on at the sparks and was also remembering his best Australian friend, Digger.

What would he have made of all this?

Digger would have probably feigned disdain and acted like it was all a big fuss about nothing.

Amble remembered that the Australians had a name for that sort of behaviour — what was it? Laconic! That was it. Digger would have been laconic!

Then Amble looked at Badger and Adele and thought how lucky he was to have such good friends, both here and in Australia.

And things got even better.

Mrs Poser decided to share her portion of pavlova with him. She so wanted to eat it all but was now seriously worried that her dress may not stay in one piece if she did.

She decided that she would eat the strawberries and meringue and let Amble have the rest.

As Amble licked cream from Mrs Poser's fingers, he thought that he was just the luckiest Labrador alive.

He had his favourite humans, his bestest friend and his big

sister here. He had Digger in Australia.
Best of all, he almost had a full tummy.
Just his favourite thing all round!

Chapter 10: Homeward Bound

After a bracing black coffee and mint chocolates, the ladies decided that they should go home — it was quite late. Also, Mr Helpful and Harriet had a lot of clearing up to do.

Mrs Pullalong called the taxi, which arrived after a few minutes. The short wait gave the ladies a chance to put on their coats as it was now quite chilly outside. As the dogs barked their farewells, the grey people carrier arrived.

It took only a few more minutes to get both ladies and dogs settled and then they set off.

"That was a lovely evening," said Mrs Poser as the taxi went around the roundabout and started to drive along the next stretch of road.

It had indeed been a lovely evening. Both ladies and dogs were pleasantly full. As the taxi drove on, they were all starting to feel deliciously sleepy.

Suddenly, the taxi screeched to a halt, waking everyone up. Thank goodness they were all fastened in otherwise they would have been thrown all over the place!

"What on earth has happened?" asked Mrs Pullalong to the taxi driver.

"I am so sorry, Madam, but there is a sheep standing just there. Right in my path. If I hadn't braked as I did, I would have knocked it over and killed it. Look — it is still standing there!"

The ladies peered through the windows and into the gloom. Only a few feet away from them was a large white sheep bleating loudly.

"There must be something wrong," observed Mrs Pullalong. "The sheep would have run away by now if there wasn't!"

"You are right!" agreed Mrs Poser. "We need to investigate!"

They asked the taxi driver to pull over. He agreed quite readily — it was his last fare of the night, and the longer he stayed out like this, the more money he would collect as his fare. So, he really didn't object to waiting while his crazy passengers got out and looked around. After all, he would be parked safely at the side of the road and with his hazard warning lights on. If any other vehicle came along, they would see him in good time. No, he was safe and earning an added bonus because of this unexpected development.

Mrs Poser rummaged in her handbag and pulled out a tiny torch.

"I always carry this in case of emergencies," she explained. "I remember when the cats went missing and we needed a torch to find them. Since then, I have always been prepared!"

Mrs Pullalong remembered how the cats had disappeared shortly after Mrs Poser had moved to her new home. She also remembered how she and Mrs Poser had searched high and low for the little beasts, without success, until long after night had fallen. Then the little blighters were discovered hiding under the garden shed. Had Mrs Poser not had her torch with her then, the cats could have been stuck under the shed all night!

The ladies made sure that Amble and Badger were safely on their leads. The ladies and dogs then set off. They walked round to the front of the car and looked at the sheep. It didn't run off. Instead, it looked at them in a commanding way then started to walk slowly away from them.

Mrs Poser said, "I think she wants us to follow her!"

They did.

The sheep led them up and over the grass verge and across a dry ditch. Thank goodness it wasn't raining. Otherwise, Mrs

Poser's shoes would have been quite ruined.

It was quite difficult to see where they were heading. The torch only gave out a narrow beam of light, but the ladies could just make out the shape of the sheep ahead. The sheep was still bleating.

Mrs Pullalong suddenly stopped.

"Did you hear that?" she asked Mrs Poser in a whisper.

Mrs Poser listened. First, she heard the sheep bleating then almost immediately after, a quieter, more timid reply.

"Come on," said Mrs Pullalong. "I think I know why the sheep was in the middle of the road!"

The two dogs led the way. They didn't need the torch to show them where to go. They could smell their way. And they knew exactly what the ladies would find — if they didn't trip up first!

The dogs guided the ladies through a hole in a fence. Mrs Poser was ever so glad that the dogs were still on the lead; otherwise, she doubted that she would have seen the hole — never mind the barbed wire which was strung almost lazily across it.

As they all navigated the fence, the timid noises became louder.

Badger stopped pulling on her lead. She turned to Amble and said, "The ladies need to look down there!"

Amble's eyes followed the direction in which Badger's nose was pointing and saw what she had found.

There was a deep dip in the land just in front of them. The sheep was standing right by its edge. And there at the bottom, was a small lamb. The dogs could see that its front leg was tangled up in barbed wire.

That was why the sheep had stopped the car. It had needed help to rescue its little one.

Mrs Pullalong realised that Badger had stopped pulling on her lead.

She turned to Mrs Poser and said, "Shine your torch down there! I think that's what we have been looking for!"

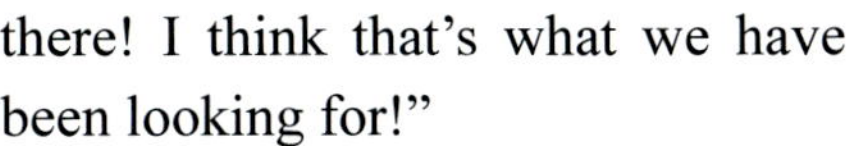

The ladies shone the torch downwards and immediately saw the tangled lamb.

Mrs Poser asked Mrs Pullalong to hold the torch.

She was going to go down!

"Be careful" cried Mrs Pullalong, as Mrs Poser scrambled down the slope into the dip.

Mrs Poser didn't care tuppence for her posh dress now. It probably had grass stains on it by now any way.

All that mattered was to try and help this poor little creature.

As Mrs Pullalong held the torch steady, Mrs Poser could see how the lamb had managed to get itself into this mess. Perhaps more importantly, she thought she could see a way that she might be able to help it.

What neither she or Mrs Pullalong had thought about at that point was what were they going to do once the sheep and lamb were reunited.

They couldn't just leave them go into the dark. The sheep could be in completely the wrong field. Or even worse, the little lamb might have some nasty injuries to its leg.

No matter, the first priority was to get rid of that horrible barbed wire. Nasty stuff!

The lamb was either so scared or so glad help had arrived

that it stayed quite still as Mrs Poser wrestled with the vicious metal string of spikes.

All the while, Mama Sheep stood at the top of the dip bleating quietly, almost soothingly, to her little one.

Fortunately, it wasn't as bad as it had at first appeared.

"Right — I think that is the last piece of wire out!" said Mrs Poser as she removed the final barb.

"Now what do we do?" asked Mrs Pullalong.

The dogs sat down. They were okay. They could stay here all night. It was dry, and they had full (or almost full in Amble's case) tummies.

Mrs Pullalong had an idea.

"Can you keep hold of the lamb?" she asked Mrs Poser.

Mrs Poser confirmed that she could and would.

"Do you have your mobile phone with you?"

Mrs Poser confirmed that she did.

"I will take the dogs back to the taxi, and then I will phone the RSPCA to get some advice! When I have done that, I will call you to let you know what is going to happen next."

Mrs Poser agreed that this was a sensible thing to do and urged Mrs Pullalong to hurry up. Mama Sheep was starting to want her baby back! The last thing anyone wanted was for the sheep to try and come down into the dip and risk getting caught up in the barbed wire!

Mrs Pullalong and the dogs rushed back to the taxi. She hastily explained what was going on, then pulled out her mobile phone, found the emergency number of the RSPCA, and called.

After several rings, a sleepy voice answered. Mrs Pullalong relayed what had happened. They had found a sheep in the middle of the road. They had had to stop. Then, they had found the sheep's lamb. And now, Mrs Poser was stuck down a dip with a lamb in her lap.

Not to mention that it was getting late, they were in a taxi and the driver wanted to be home before midnight!

The voice on the other end of the phone woke up immediately. Mrs Pullalong could tell that the person it belonged to was springing into life. This was precisely the sort of situation that the RSPCA had people on call for!

The owner of the voice would come out to them immediately — although it might take half an hour or so.

Mrs Pullalong asked the driver if he could wait another

30 minutes. Of course, he could. At this rate, he wouldn't need to work for the rest of the week. This was turning into a better fare than driving all the way to London and back!

Mrs Pullalong then rang Mrs Poser and told her to stay there in the dip with the lamb.

She confirmed that the dogs were safe and back in the taxi, and most importantly, someone from the RSPCA would come as quickly as he could.

In the event, it only took the man from the RSPCA a little over 20 minutes to find the taxi.

Mrs Pullalong and the dogs guided the Man-from-the-RSPCA from the taxi back to the top of the dip.

Now the man from the RSPCA had to decide what to do next. Luckily, this is what the RSPCA had trained him to do.

He took charge.

First, he put a lead around the sheep's neck. The sheep wasn't keen on the idea and even less keen when he tried to lead her away.

So, he went to plan B. He asked Mrs Pullalong to hold onto the lead instead.

Mrs Pullalong wasn't too enthusiastic about holding a lead to a sheep, as well as holding both dogs but there wasn't really any other option.

She was just very grateful that the two dogs seemed totally bored with what was going on and didn't seem to care two hoots that their companion was a sheep.

Meanwhile, the man from the RSPCA climbed down to

Mrs Poser.

He asked if she could stand while holding the lamb. She said that she could and did so. He then pushed her — rather inelegantly it has to be said — up to the top of the dip.

He followed, then took the lamb from her. He told Mrs Pullalong to hand the sheep and lead to Mrs Poser. The sheep would go with her.

They all made their way back to the RSPCA van which was parked behind the taxi.

Mrs Pullalong and the dogs led the way.

The taxi driver came to see what was going on.

The little lamb was now really frightened.

All it wanted to do was to run away and so it was wriggling a lot. However, the man from the RSPCA held the lamb firmly but gently. He carefully looked for injuries using the van headlights to see by.

"There doesn't seem to be a lot wrong with the little fellow," he reported. "But we can't leave the sheep and lamb here. I will have to take them back to the animal centre and the vet will check them out properly tomorrow morning."

He then handed a card to Mrs Pullalong, and one to the taxi driver and continued,

"Here is my phone number. Call me tomorrow and I can let you know what happens!"

He guided the sheep up a ramp which he had pulled out from the back of the van and into a large cage (which smelt to the sheep as if it had been recently vacated by a very large dog!).

Then he gently placed her lamb next to her.

Everyone had tears in their eyes as they watched Mama Sheep first smell then lick her child, and the lamb looking up at Mama!

Amble looked at Badger, and she at him.

Badger said to Amble, "I am so glad we were able to help! Who knows what might have happened if the taxi driver had decided to drive round the sheep!"

Amble was thinking exactly the same thing.

Mrs Poser and Mrs Pullalong were eager to get home.

Their lovely evening had been extended by an adventure. It was now very late, and they were both very tired, and Mrs Poser wanted to get out of her dress.

The taxi pulled up at Mrs Poser's house and she and Amble almost fell out of the car.

"How much do we owe you?" she asked.

After all, this journey had turned out to be a lot more complicated than simply transporting two ladies and two dogs to Mr Helpful's house.

She braced herself as the taxi driver replied.

Much to her and Mrs Pullalong's delight and amazement, he said, "I will only charge you for the trips to and from Mr Helpful's house. It was my honour to help you rescue that tiny lamb. I think I shall remember how glad it was to be reunited with its mother for the rest of my life. But may I ask that when you need a taxi again, you call me first! You ladies have such exciting lives!"

The ladies happily agreed, but insisted that he accepted a huge tip.

As Mrs Pullalong and Badger continued their journey home, Mrs Poser turned to Amble and patted him.

"You have been such a good dog tonight. Without you and Badger, I hate to think what might have happened. I know I shouldn't, but I am going to give you a treat, then we can go to bed and sleep the sleep of the well fed and righteous!"

Amble agreed totally with the idea of bed and a treat. He wasn't too sure what the 'righteous' was about, but if it meant food, he was happy.

What a day! A slap-up meal, and adventure, and no chef's whites.

Quite honestly, Amble thought it had all worked out to be his favourite thing!

Chapter 11: The Morning After

Mrs Poser and Mrs Pullalong — together with Badger and Amble of course — had set off on their usual circuit of the Wild Open Plains.

It was a glorious day with a hint of frost in the air.

The grass was long and very wet — just how the dogs liked it.

Not surprisingly, they had dashed on ahead, jumping and chasing the swallows (Badger) and sniffing the morning dew (Amble).

Following on behind, the two ladies were chatting about the previous evening's events.

They had briefly discussed the meal and agreed that it had been absolutely splendid.

They had also agreed that it had been just as well that the portion size had been so small.

By going-home time, neither Mrs Poser or Mrs Pullalong could have manged to eat another thing! Not that they wouldn't have tried. That chef was something else!

"I wonder what happened to the sheep and lamb," pondered Mrs Pullalong.

"It was a bit of a shock to see the mother in the middle of

the road like that!" observed Mrs Poser.

"Indeed," agreed Mrs Poser. "I wonder how they are getting on?"

Both ladies agreed that they wanted to find out what had happened to the woolly family.

They decided that when they got back, they would call the man from the RSPCA.

After all, he had given them his number.

Once through Mrs Poser's kitchen door, the ladies threw off their coats.

Mrs Poser put the kettle on as Mrs Pullalong found the telephone number in her coat pocket.

As they waited for the kettle to boil, Mrs Poser dialled the number. After a couple rings, it was answered. She quickly explained why she was calling then listened.

As she listened, she began to smile.

"What's happening?" asked Mrs Pullalong.

Mrs Poser put the phone down.

"That was the man from the RSPCA. The taxi driver has beaten us to it! It seems our taxi driver also wants to find out how things are going. He is going to go over there this afternoon. He is going to ring us to see if we want to join him!"

"It was a very good taxi, with so much room," observed Mrs Pullalong. "We could almost fit a school trip in there!"

Which gave Mrs Poser an idea.

Without further ado, she picked up the phone again and called the taxi driver.

First, she asked if he could confirm that he was planning to go to the RSPCA later than day.

He confirmed that he was.

She then asked if he would be willing to take Mrs Pullalong and herself as well as the dogs.

He confirmed that he was.

Mrs Poser then asked if he would be able to fit in a couple more passengers.

Would he have room?

He confirmed that he did. `

"Madam, my taxi is a people carrier. I can legally carry eight passengers — they can be adults, or children as well as the dogs."

"Thank you. I will call you back in a moment!"

She put the phone down and told Mrs Pullalong her thoughts.

Mrs Poser knew that her grandchildren were playing with their friend George at number five. Mrs Poser wondered whether she might ask them, as well as the lady from number five to come to the animal centre with them.

"I know the children would love to visit the animal centre, and if we all go there should be enough of us to make sure that neither the dogs nor the children can get into too much trouble!"

Mrs Pullalong thought that this was a simply excellent idea.

The ladies put the leads on the dogs, forgot about their tea, and rushed over to the lady from number five's house.

The lady from number five was surprised, but pleased to see them. She invited them in and shouted for the children to come and say hello. That Baby and That Other Baby rushed to their Nonna and almost knocked her over. George, however, was more polite. He held out his hand for Mrs Pullalong to shake. Then he patted each dog in turn before turning to Mrs Poser to greet her.

The ladies explained why they had arrived unannounced.

First, they told the story about how they had been to Mr Helpful's house for a slap-up dinner (more about that later they added as an aside to the lady from number five).

Then how, on the way back, they had been stopped by a sheep in the middle of the road.

The children listened in amazement as the tale about the little lamb was told.

That Baby was almost crying as Mrs Pullalong ended by saying,

"…then the man from the RSPCA came and took Mama Sheep and the lamb to the animal centre!"

"What happened then?" George wanted to know.

As the children clustered around Mrs Pullalong demanding to know more, Mrs Poser quietly took the lady from number five to one side.

She said, "The taxi driver is going to the animal centre this afternoon. He is going to call round and take us, but I checked and if you wanted to, you and the children could come with us as well!"

The lady from number five thought that this was a great idea. To be perfectly honest, she had been wondering how she was going to keep the children amused for very much longer. A trip to the animal centre, with Mrs Poser and Mrs Pullalong to help would make things so much easier!"

Of course, the lady from number five needed to check with Mrs Poser's daughter that it would be okay for That Baby and That Other Baby to go.

She rang Mrs Poser's daughter to ask.

It was okay, and even better, Mrs Poser's daughter agreed to drive over to the animal centre and meet everyone there.

This was developing into a proper afternoon out!

The taxi driver arrived at Mrs Poser's house at two o'clock prompt. As soon as everyone was fastened in their seatbelts (or restraints if you were a dog), he set off.

The animal centre was on the other side of town, quite a distance away. It took more than a little while to get there. The children were so excited though and they were there before they had a chance to get bored.

The man from the RSPCA was waiting in the car park as the fully loaded taxi drew in. He waved, and the children pressed their noses against the vehicle's windows and waved back.

Mrs Poser smiled to herself and thought that she must remember to wipe the windows down before they returned home. There was nothing like children's noses pressed against windows for smearing them! She was sure that the taxi driver wouldn't be too happy with smeary windows.

After the taxi driver had parked, everyone alighted.

The man from the RSPCA introduced himself properly.

"Hello everyone!" he said in a deep growly but not unpleasant voice, "I was last night's sheep rescuer, but my real name is George!"

That Baby looked at him and said, "My friend here is called George as well!"

That Other Baby looked across from George to George and jumped up and down with impatience. He didn't care what they were called. He wanted to meet the lamb!

George from the RSPCA took the little group into a large office. As he did so, the group introduced themselves. George remembered Mrs Poser and Mrs Pullalong, the taxi driver and the dogs from the previous night. He now knew George. The lady from number five told him that her name was Dory.

The dogs looked at each other — the lady from number five had a name!

George asked the dogs and children to sit in front of his desk (he also mentioned that the grown-ups could sit on the floor if they wanted to but strangely no-one took him up on that offer!).

"I thought I should tell you a little bit about who I am and what I do, then we can go and meet some of the animals that I have rescued," he began.

He turned his computer screen round so that everyone could see it, then started to show some photographs. He explained that the RSPCA was set up to stop cruelty to animals. It was something called a charity, which meant that it had to rely on donations — or gifts — from people who cared about animals.

George told them how the charity was first set up in the olden days — even before Nonna was born.

That Baby and That Other Baby couldn't quite believe that! Surely nothing could be older than their Nonna?

However, since it was set up, it had saved the lives of millions of animals.

Just as he was finishing his talk, there was a knock at the door. It was Mrs Poser's daughter, and she had crisps, pop, and a flask of tea with her.

Instead of setting off to look at the animals straightaway, everything was paused so they could all enjoy the refreshments.

The dogs enjoyed a bowl of mineral water. "It was all they had left at the corner shop," explained Mrs Poser's daughter in a whisper.

The children tucked into crisps and drank the fizzy pop. "I thought they would enjoy a treat!" Mrs Poser's daughter added to her mother.

The adults refreshed themselves with cups of tea.

When everyone had finished drinking and eating and the resulting mess tidied away, they all set off, with George leading the way.

The group entered the first shed. It was lined on either side with cages, and in each cage was a dog who looked both lonely and loveable.

"All these dogs are looking for someone to love them," explained George. "But we have to be very careful and make sure that they go to good homes."

"What's a good home?" asked young George.

"It's one where the people who live there know how to look after a dog. It's also very important that the home is big enough. You would be surprised at how many people want to adopt a dog but live in tiny homes that are really even too small even for them, never mind a dog!" explained George from the RSPCA.

"You must also be able to have the time to take dogs out and exercise them as well!" added Mrs Pullalong. "Badger would not be at all happy if I didn't take her out twice a day!"

Mrs Poser nodded her agreement. Even though Amble wasn't as lively as Badger, he also enjoyed his two walks a day.

Badger and Amble exchanged looks. They hadn't realised just how complicated it was to live with a human.

But they both agreed that they had landed on their paws with Mrs Poser and Mrs Pullalong.

Meanwhile, the group exited the first shed and went into the second. This one was full of smaller cages and the sounds of plaintive mewing. It was where all the cats who needed new homes were.

Amble and Badger felt sad.

They could understand everything that the cats were saying.

Some were telling the story of how they came to be there.

Others were begging to be taken home.

The dogs wanted to get out of there as quickly as they could. The children, however, had other ideas.

George, in particular, was looking at a bedraggled thin cat that looked like he had been in the wars (or at least a fight or two).

"Can you tell me about this cat?" he asked George from the RSPCA.

"This cat is Feisty Fred. He is one of our longest residents. He has been here for over a year now! No-one seems to want him. Not when they can have pretty kittens, or fluffy plump cats He can also be a bit grumpy," came the reply.

Amble leaned closer to Badger and whispered in her ear "That sounds a lot like Wafter to me!"

Badger agreed.

Nevertheless, George seemed very taken with Feisty Fred.

As the group moved on, Amble noticed that George and his mother were lagging behind and that George was talking quietly.

"I wonder what that is all about," Amble muttered to Badger.

Badger replied, "I am not too sure. But if I am right, I think we might be getting a new resident in our street soon and Wafter won't be too happy!!

By this time, the group had arrived at a small paddock where larger animals were grazing.

At one end there was an old donkey, "Who was rescued from seaside rides!" explained George from the RSPCA and an old goat, "Who will eat anything and everything, so don't stand too close."

On the far side of the paddock was Mama Sheep and her little lamb. Mama Sheep was contentedly eating the grass as the lamb frisked about her. It was a lovely sight.

"Goodness me," said the taxi driver. "They have recovered quickly! I wouldn't have given tuppence for the lamb's chances last night!"

"Indeed," agreed George from the RSPCA. "It is truly amazing how quickly our animal friends can get better if they are treated with a little kindness!"

As he spoke, he felt a gentle tap on his back. It was young George.

"Please, Sir," he asked. "Can my mummy ask you something?"

"Of course!" came the reply, and George from the RSPCA moved from the front of the group to where Dory was standing.

Badger moved closer too. She wanted to know what was going on. As she listened, she realised that her suspicions were correct.

Dory had agreed that young George could indeed adopt Feisty Fred, but only if the RSPCA allowed them to. Now she wanted to know what she had to do so that they could.

George from the RSPCA explained that he would have to come and look at her house and make sure it was suitable for a cat, and to check that young George understood what he had to do. Adopting a cat was a huge responsibility.

Dory agreed a time and date with George from the RSPCA and re-joined the group.

By now, the group had seen everything at the animal centre.

Mrs Pullalong and the taxi driver thanked George from the RSPCA for his time and prepared to leave.

That Baby and That Other Baby climbed into their car seats in their mother's car.

Everyone else returned to the taxi. As they did so, George ran after them. He was waving a piece of paper.

He ran up to the Dory, handed the paper to her and said, "Here is my telephone number. Call me if you need to discuss anything!"

"I presume he's talking about Feisty Fred," said Mrs Poser.

"I'm not too sure," replied Mrs Pullalong. "I think we might have the start of a romance on our hands!"

Badger and Amble looked at each other. Now there was something they hadn't expected from this trip. A new cat was one thing. But a new romance as well?

Amble wasn't too sure what a romance might be. However, he was sure he would find out soon and who knows? Watching one happen could be one of his favourite things!

Chapter 12: Developments

Over the next few weeks, an awful lot seemed to happen.

Mrs Poser and Mrs Pullalong watched the developments with fascination.

The two dogs were equally curious.

There was a new cat on the block. Feisty Fred had arrived.

Wafter had been downright nervous — she had only just established herself as Top Cat. If Amble was to be believed, her superior position was now threatened by some interloper. And all because of a slap-up dinner.

The three kittens couldn't have cared less what was happening. They were far too busy chasing butterflies and dandelion seeds to worry about anything.

As the ladies sat eating ginger biscuits and drinking yet another cup of tea, Mrs Pullalong observed, "The RSPCA van has visited Number Five a lot this week."

"I noticed that too!" replied Mrs Poser. "Do you suppose that Feisty Fred isn't settling down?"

"I'm not too sure that it's Feisty Fred that is being visited,"

Mrs Pullalong continued. "Unless he has a taste for flowers and chocolates!"

"What??" exclaimed Mrs Poser.

"Oh yes — and there's more…"

Meanwhile, Amble and Badger were talking with Wafter. They wanted to know if she had met Feisty Fred yet, and perhaps more importantly, whether he lived up to his name. If he was a feisty as his name suggested, Wafter might have a problem on her paws!

It did indeed appear that Wafter had brushed tails with Feisty Fred.

They had entered into peace talks straight away.

Wafter had discovered that Fred wasn't feisty at all.

In fact, he was rather lovely and laid back. He had even made friends with the kittens and was doing a great job of keeping them out of her fur.

He was quite happy to stay in his garden and entertain the kittens when they wandered in.

Both he and Wafter had agreed that there was plenty of room for them both on the Wild Open Plains. There was no need to fight over who could go where, just so long as they did so at different times.

Most importantly, Fred didn't want any new responsibilities — he just wanted to enjoy his newfound freedom. After all, he had been in a cage at the animal centre for far too long.

No, he was perfectly happy to let Wafter be Top Cat as long as she didn't bother him.

It was all good.

"So why is the George still calling round?" asked Amble.

Badger sniffed, and then said, "You aren't very observant, are you? It was perfectly clear to me when we went to the animal centre that the George took a shine to the Dory!"

"Really?" exclaimed Amble, who hadn't noticed anything of the sort.

"Oh yes. Didn't you notice how he introduced himself as George? And then how we found out that the lady from number five has a name because she told him in front of us?"

"I remember that I was surprised that she had a name…" said Amble carefully, "It reminded me of a fish. Dory, wasn't it?"

"Yes, that's right," agreed Badger. "And don't you

remember that when we first met George, he had a beard and rather untidy hair?"

"Yes…"

"And have you seen him now? No beard and tidy hair?"

"Yes…" agreed Amble, who was still confused.

"Well," said Badger, who was starting to get more than a little exasperated with her canine friend. "He didn't do that for Fred! He didn't do it for little George and he certainly didn't do it for George's guinea pig!"

"So why did he do it, then?" asked Amble who was now really confused.

Badger almost gave up at this point. Then, she took a deep breath, and stated what seemed to be perfectly obvious to her.

"I think that the lady from number five and George from the RSPCA are having a romance!"

As she told Amble this, she quietly prayed to herself that she would not have to explain what a romance was. That would be too much!

Fortunately for Badger's patience (which was at breaking point), Amble did understand… sort of.

But then he asked, "So what does this mean?"

Badger gave up.

"I don't know," she replied.

Meanwhile, the ladies were also still pondering developments at number five. They, too, had noticed George's transformation. They both agreed that he had scrubbed up rather well.

Mrs Poser mused, "If I were twenty years younger…"

"You still wouldn't have got a look in!" completed Mrs Pullalong.

Both ladies decided that they needed to find out more about the developments at number five. It was all so intriguing.

As they finished their tea and got ready for the dog walk, they both decided that they should invite Dory round for tea and biscuits so that they could find out more.

"But we will have to be subtle!" said Mrs Pullalong as they strode across the Wild Open Plains.

"Oh yes!" agreed Mrs Poser.

Both the dogs, who had been running ahead, heard this exchange and stopped in their tracks.

Those two ladies couldn't be subtle if they tried!

Both Badger and Amble decided that they would have to forego their playtime in the garden when the tea party happened. They wanted to watch the ladies trying to be subtle.

This could be fun, and definitely their favourite thing!

Chapter 13: Amazing

It took the ladies quite some time to organise Dory to come to tea. It was important that they quizzed her without Little George being there.

But it seemed that every time the ladies were free, either Dory was doing the school run, or George was calling. It was very frustrating.

But this mystery was too good to stop the ladies trying to sort out the tea party.

Thanks to their perseverance, they eventually managed to get Dory into Mrs Poser's kitchen and seated at the table.

Mrs Pullalong poured the tea.

Mrs Poser offered her ginger biscuits and added, "They were freshly baked this morning!"

The dogs were settled under the table. They had waited a long time for this meeting to happen. They wanted to watch the ladies trying to be subtle.

Meanwhile, the kittens had all disappeared outside as it was a lovely day for hunting.

"Your new cat seems to have settled in well," said Mrs Pullalong to open the conversation.

"And he seems to be getting on rather well with my four!" added Mrs Poser. "I was afraid that there might have been trouble when Fred moved in, but they all seem to be getting on just fine. The kittens love him."

"Indeed," agreed Dory. "They play so nicely with Fred

when they come into our garden. They chase his tail and lick him, and he doesn't seem to mind at all!"

The dogs looked at each other. This was all too polite and general.

Mrs Poser and Mrs Pullalong couldn't keep this up for much longer, could they?

There was a brief lull in the conversation as the ladies all nibbled their respective ginger biscuits, then Mrs Poser couldn't contain herself any more.

She put down her half-eaten biscuit, brushed the crumbs from around her mouth and said, "You know, I couldn't help but notice that the RSPCA van is here an awful lot. Is Fred ill?"

Mrs Pullalong smothered a nervous giggle.

The two dogs sat up and were now fully alert. Things were definitely starting to get interesting.

Dory didn't appear to mind the question at all. In fact, her expression became quite dreamy and wistful.

"I really need to thank you for organising that trip to the animal centre," she said. "You helped me amuse three boisterous children that day, and George found a new pet. And…"

Mrs Poser and Mrs Pullalong were now on the edge of their seats.

"Go on," urged Mrs Pullalong

"…I wouldn't have met George from the RSPCA otherwise!"

Ah — ha!

Badger had been right. She knew she was!

Now that Dory had started to talk about George, it was impossible for the two ladies to get a word in edgeways.

But they did find out an awful lot.

The dogs settled down to listen. This was going to take a lot longer than they had expected. There were many things to discuss.

First of all, the ladies learnt that Dory had moved here with Little George and Percy the guinea pig shortly after Little George's father had died. It had been so very sad. In fact, it turned out that Percy the guinea pig had been a present from Little George's father just before he died. Percy was very precious to Little George.

When Percy had disappeared, Little George had been beside himself.

Amble realised that finding the guinea pig in the long grass had been far more important to Little George than he had ever realised. Thank goodness Amble had found him.

Not only had it led to Amble and Mrs Poser meeting Dory and Little George, Amble had been able to unite a little boy with a precious link to his father.

The ladies sipped their tea sympathetically as Dory had told them how lonely she had been. It was so difficult to be both mummy and daddy to Little George. For a start, she was hopeless at football!

Moving here had been such a good idea.

Little George had settled well at school as well.

It was just perfect that he was best friends with Mrs Poser's grandchildren. Not to mention Sammy from just up the road.

Everything was good.

And then, things got even better.

By now, the ladies were almost falling off their chairs with curiosity and excitement.

"Do go on," begged Mrs Pullalong as Mrs Poser offered another ginger biscuit.

"You remember how Little George wanted to adopt the cat?"

"Indeed," replied Mrs Poser. "It was at the animal centre."

"Don't interrupt!" commanded Mrs Pullalong who now wanted to get the rest of this story.

"At first, I thought George was just doing his job and making sure that Fred was settled. Which he was, in the early days at least."

Dory then told Mrs Poser and Mrs Pullalong how George had taken an interest in her and Little George as well as Fred.

Both she and Little George felt that was so nice to share things like sports days with him. George had even taken part in the Fathers' Race — and had come second. (He would have won, but he had been out tending to some sheep earlier in the day and still been wearing his wellington boots.)

Little George had been so proud at sports day. It was, Dory confessed, the first time that she had felt part of a proper family again, rather than just her and Little George against the world.

Things had moved quickly since that day. It became clear that George wasn't just calling round to see about the cat. More importantly, his intentions were entirely honourable.

Amble stuck an ear up at this last comment as he didn't really understand what Dory meant.

"It means that he wanted to take her out so he could get to know her better!" Badger whispered.

Amble wondered why, but not for long as he was too busy listening.

"And now, we get to the really exciting news that I have wanted to tell you about for days now, but I had to make sure that Little George was happy first…"

Now both dogs' ears pricked up.

A revelation was imminent!

Badger and Amble loved revelations.

Not that Amble really knew what such a thing might be. But if it meant people were happy and he got extra treats, he loved them with all his heart.

"George and I talked with Little George last night. Little George has given us his blessing…" Dory continued. "And I wanted you to be the first people to know as we would never have met otherwise!"

At this point, Dory put her left hand on the table. The dogs were cross as they couldn't see what was going on, but from the squeals of joy above, Badger realised what was happening.

"Tell me!" demanded Amble who still didn't have much of a clue.

"I think that George has asked Dory to marry him. And he has given her a posh ring with a sparkly stone in it to make it all official."

"Why?" asked Amble as all of this was way outside his experience.

"Because that's what humans do!" snapped back Badger who was despairing of her friend at this point.

To say that the ladies were pleased was a bit of an understatement.

Mrs Poser let out a rather undignified shout which sounded like, "Yippee!"

Mrs Pullalong scratched Badger's ear a little too roughly as she muttered, "I knew it! I just knew it!"

After a few moments, though, they calmed down and talk turned to what was going to happen next.

Mrs Poser wanted to tell her daughter straight away. Mrs Poser loved sharing good news (especially news that she had found out first!)

Mrs Pullalong had a more important question to ask.

"Where do you want to get married?" she asked and then almost as an afterthought, "Can we help?"

"That would be super," replied Dory. "This has all happened so suddenly, and I really don't have a clue where to start."

"Leave it to us!" said Mrs Pullalong. "Why don't you set out all your questions and then we can find out the answers together!"

Mrs Poser remembered when her daughter had got married. It seemed like there was no end to the preparations and details that had to be considered. Fortunately, she still had her little notebook which held lots of information from that time. It might come in handy.

She and Amble went upstairs to find the book. Mrs Pullalong and Dory stayed in the kitchen and began to work out what to ask first.

"The first thing you need is a date!" announced Mrs Poser as she came back with the notebook. "And that must be agreed with George before you do anything else! Then everything else can be decided!"

Mrs Pullalong added, "Please try to make sure there is enough time for everything to be organised. I doubt you will want a royal wedding, but there will still be an awful lot to do!"

Dory stood to leave.

"I can't thank you enough," she said, "I will talk with George tonight, and we can take things from there!"

The ladies put the dirty teacups into the sink.

Mrs Poser said, "That was a turn up for the books. Well done you for spotting that one!"

"And haven't the dogs been good?" replied Mrs Pullalong. "It was almost like they were listening!"

Amble and Badger looked at each other. Didn't they realise? That was exactly what they had been doing, and now they had news to share with the cats and Adele.

"Yes," agreed Mrs Poser. "Let's take them for a walk as a reward!"

Amble and Badger barked with joy. They had exciting news to share with the cats and Adele and now they were going for a walk as well.

It couldn't get any better — could it?

Both dogs agreed that watching the ladies being subtle could be another of their favourite things!

Chapter 14: Preparations

Ever since that fateful cup of tea, there seemed to be no time to rest up.

George and Dory had set the date for their wedding and had even decided on where they wanted to be married.

That meant that many other decisions could now be made, plans put into place, and arrangements made.

Wafter watched as Mrs Poser read through yet another issue of Bride magazine, and said to Amble,

"I really can't understand why this wedding is causing so much excitement! You would think it was Mrs Poser who was getting married for all the effort she is putting into it. Honestly, I think that if you hadn't have reminded her by knocking over your food bowl, she might have even forgotten to feed us!"

Amble agreed.

Mrs Poser had become very distant and preoccupied these days. Not that Mrs Pullalong was any different.

Both Amble and Badger agreed that walks with the ladies were even starting to become a little boring.

Since the announcement, the ladies had taken to walking up to the nearest bench, sitting on it and chatting among themselves. The dogs either sat around, sniffed the hedgerow or if totally bored, chased a few seagulls. There wasn't a ball or stick to be thrown.

All the dogs could do was hope that the wedding would happen soon, and then things might just get back to normal.

Amble and Wafter sat side by side and watched morosely as Mrs Poser read on. She occasionally paused to sip the ever-present cup of tea balanced precariously on the arm of her chair. Then she would mutter odd words to herself.

Amble remembered the last time he had witnessed similar behaviour. It had been when they had moved to a new house. He hadn't listened carefully then and had been very confused about what was happening. However, Amble had learnt from that experience, and now he was holding onto her every word — even though most of them didn't seem to make much sense. If he could remember them, he could ask Badger for help later.

Over at Mrs Pullalong's house, Badger was observing similar behaviour.

It was all very odd.

Humans could be very strange sometimes.

Both Mrs Poser and Mrs Pullalong felt that it was vital that they paid attention to every detail, no matter how trivial. Even simple weddings were full of things that could go wrong.

It was important that Dory's special day was perfect.

Dory and Little George had had a few, very hard years. Now there was a chance to have real happiness again.

This wedding would mark the first day in the next part of her life.

There was sudden knock at Mrs Poser's door.

Mrs Poser jumped up, almost knocking her cup to the floor.

Thank goodness it was empty.

Wafter ran for cover as Amble ran to the door to bark at it.

It was Mr Helpful and Adele.

At last, Amble had his sister with him, and they could have some fun. Much better than listening to Mrs Poser slurp and mutter.

Mr Helpful took off his coat and pulled up a chair to the table. Mrs Poser let the dogs into the back garden and then asked,

"Do I need to get Mrs Pullalong over as well?"

As she headed over to the phone, the dogs played happily outside.

"Do you know," began Adele. "Mr Helpful is behaving quite strangely!"

"I know what you mean," replied Amble. "Mrs Poser is the same. She almost forgot to feed me and the cats this morning!"

"I think it's this wedding," said Adele. "I think Mrs Poser has asked Mr Helpful for advice!"

Badger suddenly appeared from the direction of the kitchen door.

Her only words to Adele were, "You too?"

As Adele nodded, they decided that life was too short to spend too much time wondering about human behaviour. Especially when there was some serious chasing to be done!

Back inside, Mrs Pullallong had joined Mr Helpful and Mrs Poser at the kitchen table.

Wafter watched from her place of safety behind the window curtain.

"So where have we got to?"

Mrs Poser put her copy of Bride magazine on the table. Mr Helpful and Mrs Pullalong leaned forward to look.

"There!" exclaimed Mrs Poser. "Look at those flowers!

Don't you think they would make a beautiful bouquet? And we have most of those plants in our gardens, so we can make it up ourselves!"

"That would be so much cheaper than buying them from a flower shop," observed Mr Helpful.

"And we can use similar flowers from our gardens for the table displays!" added Mrs Pullalong.

"And Harriet could arrange them! She is very talented with flowers!"

Both the ladies excitedly nodded their heads in agreement.

Wafter almost fell off the window sill with disgust.

This was a wedding planning committee.

Wafter realised that she would either have to move now or stay where she was, or risk being drawn in. She didn't want to offer any advice at all. Indeed, the only advice she would be willing to give would be to stop all this fuss right now! It was all too much.

However, the sun was shining through the window, and so Wafter decided to stay put. She might learn something after all, and it was nice and warm there.

She decided to pretend to be asleep. It worked so well that within a couple of seconds, she was!

"I have some news!" announced Mr Helpful.

"Go on," urged Mrs Pullalong.

"Harriet met with Dory yesterday. It seems that Harriet has agreed to make the wedding dress!"

Both Mrs Poser and Mrs Pullalong knew that Harriet was a talented flower arranger.

But to be able to make dresses as well. This was all just too good to be true!

It would be lovely to have Harriet involved in this way! At this rate, all the friends would have important roles to play in this big day.

"And it gets even better!" continued Mr Helpful. "I have asked the chef from our slap-up meal if he would do the catering for the reception afterwards. He has agreed. And because he had such a good time with our meal, he is going to only charge for the food and not his time!"

Mrs Pullalong then reported that he had asked the taxi driver if he would help. She was pleased to report that he would be delighted to help. He had even offered to put a ribbon on the front of the taxi.

Things were starting to come together — which was just as well as there wasn't much time now until the big day.

All that was left for the wedding planners to do was to meet up with Dory. They needed to make sure that they had covered everything.

They had done as much as they could, and if it all worked out, it would be a splendid day which would be quite everyone's favourite thing to talk about for years to come!

Chapter 15: The Big Day — Part One

The wedding day had finally arrived. Was it raining?

Mrs Poser needed to know. She leapt out of bed and was so intent on looking out of the window that she almost tripped over Amble who was fast asleep at the side of the bed.

"Huh?" he grunted.

But Mrs Poser was too excited to notice.

Today was the day the lady from number five was marrying George from the RSPCA. So far, the weather was looking good, but the wedding wasn't until later.

Mrs Poser decided to get up early, head downstairs and listen to the forecast.

Amble sleepily followed her. It was still a little early for him. Mornings were not his best time. However, if Mrs Poser was up and about, he might be able to have an early breakfast.

Outside, the kittens had heard Mrs Poser in the distance and came running in through the cat flap. It had been a hard but not very successful night of hunting for them. They had only managed to catch one moth between the four of them all night!

An early breakfast would be very welcome!

Wafter stirred from her cosy nook on the sofa. It had been a lovely quiet night without the pesky youngsters to annoy her. She had slept well and was also ready for her breakfast.

As the hungry hoard clustered at her feet, Mrs Poser put the radio on. Only after that did she turn her attention to breakfast duty.

As she opened tins and spooned contents onto cat plates, she listened intently to the weather forecast. She was concentrating so hard that Amble nearly ended up with Wafter's food.

Amble was about to alert her to this criminal error (not on his part, you understand. For Amble, food was food, but Wafter could be quite particular about what she ate). But, it was good news. According to the radio, the day was going to be lovely. Not too hot, not too cold and absolutely no possibility of rain.

Mrs Poser sighed with relief, looked again at what she was about to do and stopped.

Then she gave Wafter her bowl of food and put Amble's food in front of him.

Disaster averted and situation back to normal.

After breakfast, Mrs Poser prepared for the dog walk. Amble skipped around her — he was so pleased that things were getting back to normal.

But no — instead of waiting for Mrs Pullalong, Mrs Poser shouted to Amble, and they walked round to Mrs Pullalong's house.

"It looks like it's going to be a perfect day," said Mrs Poser as the door opened.

"Indeed," said Mrs Pullalong, as she handed Badger's lead over. "Come on through. Amble and Badger can go for a romp on the Wild Open Plains!"

Badger and Amble looked at each other. This was not usual. Weren't the two ladies going to come with them?

It seemed not. Only Mrs Poser, apparently. She walked on, and the two puzzled dogs followed.

However, the day was too nice to stay bemused for long. The two dogs enjoyed a swim in the river and an excellent stick throwing session before returning to Mrs Poser's house. After a rinse with the dreaded hosepipe and a brisk towelling down, they were ready to go inside. They were a little sad that the wonderful smell of fox poo that they had acquired during one rather spontaneous roll in the grass had disappeared, but to be fair, they both felt clean and fresh now.

"There we are!" exclaimed Mrs Poser. "We will brush you both down when we get inside and then you will be ready."

Ready for what?

They went in, and the dogs were surprised again.

Mrs Pullalong was already there, but it was not Mrs Pullalong as they knew her. It was a very, very glamorous Mrs Pullalong. With her hair all styled, and she was even wearing a dress!

"I didn't realise she had legs," observed Amble.

"Neither did I," replied Badger. "And I have lived with her for longer than I can remember!"

"Thank you for taking Badger!" Mrs Pullalong said to Mrs Poser. "Now it's your turn to get ready."

The dogs watched as Mrs Poser dashed upstairs and then they waited. And waited. And waited.

After what seemed like for ever, Mrs Poser returned, but again — surprise. What a transformation.

Badger had finally put two and two together.

The wedding was today. And they were all getting ready for it.

A knock at the door! Now what?

Mrs Poser rushed to answer it.

There was the taxi driver, all done up in his best suit.

The dogs rushed out to the car. Then stopped.

What was this?

The car had a huge pink bow across its front.

This was too much. It was a wedding. That much was true. But a pink bow? That was going over the top.

But strangely, the ladies didn't appear at all perturbed by this development. Indeed, quite the opposite.

The taxi driver opened the door. The ladies got in, and noted they were only just ready in time.

The taxi driver replied that this wasn't problem. He had arrived early.

He had to take them to the wedding and then he would go and collect Dory and Little George.

The pink bow made sense now. It was for Dory: not Badger or Amble, or Mrs Poser or Mrs Pullalong either.

But Amble still felt it was a bit over the top.

Wafter and the kittens watched as the car left.

"Well," observed Wafter. "That is the last we will see of them for the rest of today!"

"I hope we will have enough food!" said Meany, who despite only just having finished breakfast, was starting to feel a tad peckish again.

"Mrs Poser has been very reliable since we arrived," observed Mo. "Let's go and check!"

The kittens turned and rushed indoors to investigate.

Wafter watched them go, and thought to herself, "I am sure we will all be well catered for. It's going to be so nice to have the house to ourselves for the whole day. I wonder what mischief I can encourage those kittens into while everyone is away? I love being Top Cat! Indeed, in the words of that pesky pooch, it could be my favourite thing!"

Chapter 16: The Big Day — Part Two

The taxi stopped outside the registry office. The ladies and dogs got out. As they went towards the door, a rather burly man in a blue uniform came towards them and put up his hand.

"No dogs allowed. Except guide dogs!"

The ladies stopped. They had to think quickly. There was no way that this wedding was going to take place without the dogs.

Mrs Poser looked at the man and said, in a very steely voice,

"Mrs Pullalong and I are the wedding planners. We need to make sure that everything is as it should be before the bride, groom and guests arrive. These two dogs are trained sniffer dogs and we want them to make sure that there are no unpleasant surprises!"

The man in the blue uniform looked at Mrs Pullalong, in her posh frock and fancy shoes, and then across to Mrs Poser in her two-piece suit and fascinator. Then he looked down to Amble and Badger.

They returned his glare with expressions that were a perfect blend of professional 'yes, we are sniffer dogs' and cute innocence.

Both dogs hoped that they would be impossible to resist.

The man in a blue suit crumbled.

"All right then!" he said. "I will let you all in, but you must promise me that you will go straight to the room where the wedding is to be held, and you won't leave until it has finished!"

"Don't worry, Sir," replied Mrs Pullalong in her most official voice. "These dogs have an important job to do. They will behave themselves!"

With that, they entered the building, followed the signs and reached the wedding room.

Only when they were safely inside, did Mrs Poser take off her fascinator and slump down on one of the chairs. Mrs Pullalong slumped beside her.

"That was close!" she said.

"Wasn't it?" agreed Mrs Poser. "But I didn't fib. Both Amble and Badger are trained, and they do enjoy sniffing…"

With that, the ladies decided that they needed to make sure everything was as it should be before the guests arrived.

The pink satin covers that had been ordered for the chairs were in place. The flowers, which had been picked the night

before, had been beautifully arranged. The lavender and peonies blended perfectly with the white sprays of small flowers which Mrs Pullalong told the dogs were called "Love in a Mist".

Although she hadn't a clue why they were called that.

"Harriet is so talented," observed Mrs Poser as she surveyed the room. "I knew she was going to come in earlier this morning to do the flowers, and they are simply gorgeous. I can't wait to see what the wedding dress looks like!"

The dogs' ears pricked up. They could hear footsteps approaching the door.

This would be a real test for them. They were all too aware that if they barked, they could be thrown out of the building. But not to bark was a direct breaking of the cardinal dog rule!

Fortunately, Mrs Pullalong had also heard the noise. She put her finger to her lips and quietly said, "Shush!"

If Mrs Pullalong had told them to be quiet and not bark then that was all right. The only time you can break a cardinal dog rule is if you are commanded by your owner to do so.

The door opened, and in marched Mr Helpful and Adele.

"We are so pleased to see you both," said Mrs Poser. "But how did you get past the front door?"

"I told that young man that Adele was a trained guide dog — which she is. He said that trained guide dogs are allowed in. Here we are!"

The next to arrive were Mrs Amin and Sammy.

Sammy had been asked to do an important job for the wedding. He had to wait by the door. When the guests arrived, he was to hand out the sheets with all the words on. Every guest had to have one. He also had one more important job. Sammy had to let Mrs Poser know when the bride and her retinue arrived.

It wasn't too long before guests started to arrive. The room was rapidly starting to fill up. Sammy was kept very busy.

Then George strode in. With him was the tallest man you have ever seen. He was apparently George's work colleague, and his best man.

Mrs Pullalong settled them both in the front row on the right-hand side.

Then Sammy came hurling down the aisle between the seats to tell Mrs Poser

"They're here!"

Mrs Poser gave a signal, and music started to play. It was very majestic and serious music. Everyone stood up.

Then the door opened, and in walked the bridesmaids, led by Harriet and Mrs Poser's daughter who were matrons of honour.

They were followed by That Baby and Ila who both looked adorably cute.

That Other Baby followed. He was dressed as a page boy and was carrying a lacy pillow which had two gold rings balanced on it. He felt a right cissy. But he had to make sure that he didn't lose the rings otherwise there would be big trouble.

Had he had his way, That Other Baby wouldn't have been

dressed like this. He would have been a Jedi knight, and the rings would have been threaded on his light sabre. There would have been no danger of them falling off and rolling away then! Unless Darth Vader arrived, of course.

Finally, Dory came in. She was wearing the most beautifully elegant mid length dress. It was powder blue and blended perfectly with her bouquet. Her escort was none other than Little George, who now had the most important job of his life — to give his mother's hand in marriage!

When they reached the front, the bridesmaids moved to the left. Mrs Poser's daughter grabbed That Other Baby's shoulder and made sure he was standing right next to her.

Little George and his mother stood at the front. George and his best man stood up and moved towards them. They all stood together in a row facing a lady with a very floaty hat. She held a book which she then opened.

The music stopped, and the ceremony began.

Amble, Adele and Badger watched with interest. They had never been to a wedding before. They weren't too sure what it was all about, but they knew it was very special and so it was important that they gave it full attention.

There was a lot of talking. First the lady in the floaty hat asked if anyone knew of any reason why the couple shouldn't marry.

Amble thought that that was all rather unnecessary. They wouldn't be here if there was.

Then she asked who was going to give Dory away.

That confused both Badger and Amble, but not Little George.

He proudly took one step forward and said in a loud clear voice, "I am!"

There was a bit more fussing about, and then the lady turned to George and asked,

"Do you, George Michael…"

Mrs Pullalong leaned across to Mrs Poser, both ladies were smiling.

"George is named after a pop star! Who would have thought that his mother was a WHAM! fan!" whispered Mrs Poser.

The ladies turned to look at his mother, who looked like

she would be more at home knitting pullovers than dancing to 1980's pop music.

"It goes to show that you can't judge by appearances," observed Mrs Pullalong.

After some more talking, the lady in the floaty hat turned to Dory.

"Do you, Dorcas Eliza…"

What?

The dogs had heard Dory introduce herself to George, but they thought her name was Dory. Where had this Dorcas Eliza come from?

There was no time to stay bemused though. Shortly after that, the lady in the floaty hat announced that George Michael and Dorcas Eliza were now man and wife. He could kiss the bride.

Now it was the children's turn to be shocked. Kissing Dory? You couldn't do that. She was old!

No matter, George kissed his bride, and then escorted her down the central aisle back out of the room. Thankfully, not to the music of WHAM!

"What happens now?" asked Badger to Adele.

Adele replied, "I think we now go for a meal — it's called a wedding breakfast. I am not sure why it's called that because it's well past lunchtime, but I do know Mr Helpful has been working hard with Chef, so let's go and find out!"

With that, Adele returned to Mr Helpful's side, and they both disappeared into the crowd of guests heading towards the door.

Chapter 17: The Big Day — Part Three

Amble's ears had pricked up at the mention of a meal. He was particularly interested if the meal was going to be prepared by the chef from the slap-up dinner. Amble still had dreams of the chicken pieces in broth.

It seemed to take forever for everyone to leave the room. The ladies decided to wait for a few minutes, so they wouldn't get caught up in the crush.

When they eventually got downstairs, Mrs Pullalong and Mrs Poser looked around. They had expected to see the newly-weds, the bridesmaids and all the guests still milling around on the steps outside the main door, but it was all completely empty apart from the taxi, parked at the bottom of the steps, and still with its huge pink bow. Even the burly man in the blue uniform had disappeared.

"Come along, ladies," shouted the taxi driver. "You are the last guests to take to the wedding breakfast. Everyone will be waiting for you!"

Badger and Amble looked at each other. The meal was indeed called a breakfast. The taxi driver had said so as well.

They wondered why the meal should be called breakfast. Surely it wasn't going to be toast and marmalade at this time of day?

The little group got into the taxi once again and put on their seat belts and restraints. The taxi set off.

Mrs Poser and Mrs Pullalong chatted amiably throughout the journey. They compared impressions and opinions on who had been there and what they had been wearing.

They commented on how lovely Dorcas Eliza had looked (they couldn't call her the lady from number five anymore. Not now they had been told her proper full name).

The bridesmaids had looked absolutely adorable.

Little George had been the perfect person to give Dorcas Eliza away.

And That Other Baby had looked so cute but very uncomfortable in his little pageboy suit.

The ladies felt that Harriet had excelled herself. Not only had she decorated the room with flowers (and made the bouquet), she had put so much work into making all the dresses and outfits.

The dogs were completely bored by this conversation. Yet they had to listen to it. They couldn't do anything else because they were stuck in their restraints and in the taxi. They both hoped that this journey wouldn't be too long.

Fortunately, it didn't.

"That was quick!" said Mrs Poser as the taxi stopped.

As they got out, all of a tumble, the dogs realised where they were.

They were at the animal centre.

"This is a strange place for a breakfast!" observed Amble.

"Indeed, but it is where the happy couple first met,"

replied Badger.

Meanwhile, Mrs Pullalong was walking briskly through the entrance and up towards the office where they had all listened to George Michael telling them about the RSPCA.

Mrs Poser wasn't too far behind.

The dogs supposed that they had better follow or they might get left behind. Or even worse, be mistaken for strays. It was the animal centre after all. Both dogs remembered the large hall lined with cages full of lost or unwanted dogs.

Neither Amble or Badger wanted to be in one of those cages.

When they reached the office, the dogs couldn't believe their eyes. It didn't look like an office at all anymore. The desks and computers were nowhere to be seen. Even the large white photocopier had disappeared.

Instead, there were tables and chairs and flowers and balloons, and a huge banner which hung over the table at the end of the room, which said, "Congratulations George and Dorcas."

Mrs Poser and Mrs Pullalong made their way over to one of the tables where Mr Helpful, Harriet and Adele were already seated. At the next table was Mrs Poser's daughter, together with

the two gorgeous grandchildren, and Mrs Amin with Sammy and Ila.

Badger looked around. All the other tables, except the one at the end of the room were occupied.

As the dogs settled down, music started to play, and a loud voice boomed, "Please stand and welcome our newly-weds."

The doors opened and in walked the happy couple and Little George.

Everyone cheered and clapped. Badger wasn't too keen on this display. She hid under the table next to Mrs Pullalong's feet.

Amble and Adele simply watched and waited. After all, they had been trained not to be worried by strange noises or human activities. Even if he hadn't passed his guide dog test, Amble still remembered most of what he was supposed to do. Being able to ignore all the noise also gave him and Adele the chance to watch what was going on.

Amble looked around. There was a huge cake on the table at the front. It was covered in icing and looked delicious. Amble so wanted to find out if it was a good as it looked. Mrs Poser saw him eying it up and told him a very stern "No!" Amble felt that Mrs Poser was being a spoilsport, and he slunk under the table to join Badger.

When the happy couple and Little George reached the table, they told everyone to sit down. It had been a wonderful day so far, but they were now hungry.

Amble looked out from under the table. As he watched, more food than he could have imagined was put on all the tables.

He nudged Badger, who was still trying to hide under Mrs Pullalong's strappy shoes.

"Come out, Badger! It's safe now. And you won't believe how much food there is!" he told his black and white friend.

All three dogs now had rumbling tummies as they watched more and more food being taken past them then, as if someone in the kitchen (Chef perhaps? He was their friend after all) knew what they were thinking, three bowls of delicious chicken pieces in broth were placed on the floor next to them.

Deep, deep joy! Just the same taste as the slap-up meal. The dogs forgot about everything else that was happening around them and tucked in with enthusiasm.

In between slurps, all three of them agreed it was just their favourite thing.

As the meal drew to close, Mrs Pullalong leaned across to Mrs Poser and muttered, "There are going to be speeches now. There always are!"

"I hope they aren't too long," agreed Mrs Poser. "I am not sure Amble will keep still if they are."

Sure enough, as these words were uttered, George Michael stood up and began to speak.

"Hello, everyone," he began. "Thank you so much for coming. This is the most special day of my life so far, and I am so pleased you could share it with me."

"That's nice," commented Mrs Poser to no-one in particular.

George Michael continued, "I want to thank my lovely bride for agreeing to marry me."

"Just as well she did after we went to all this effort," muttered Mrs Pullalong.

"I want to thank Little George for allowing me to marry his beautiful mother…"

Dorcas Eliza blushed!

"And her beautiful bridesmaids…"

Now Harriet and Mrs Poser's daughter blushed. That Baby and Ila couldn't have cared less. They had wandered off and discovered a huge chocolate fountain at the back of the room.

"I couldn't not mention our handsome ring bearer either…"

That Other Baby glowered at George Michael. Not that he noticed. He still had more people to thank.

"And I want to thank all of her friends for all the hard work and talent that has made all of this possible!"

"First of all, I want to say a big thank you to Harriet. She decorated both the room where we were married and here as well. She made all the dresses. It was a lot of hard work, but definitely worthwhile…"

"I want to thank chef and Mr Helpful for the wonderful food. None of us had time or energy for food before the wedding. When we came in here, we were very hungry. The food was magnificent. The cake is amazing!"

Amble wholeheartedly agreed with that last part. That cake looked SO good.

Meanwhile, Badger had worked out why this meal was called a wedding breakfast. Because the wedding was so special, people didn't want to eat before it; however, once it was over, they were starving.

It was the first meal of the day for so many people.

Now it made sense.

George Michael was still thanking everyone — his best man for his support, Sammy for handing out the words, until he concluded,

"Finally, I would like to thank Mrs Poser and Mrs Pullalong for all their help. I understand that they are superb organisers. But, most

importantly, if it hadn't been for them, I would never have met my beautiful wife and none of this would have happened!"

Now it was the ladies' turn to blush.

At this point, everyone in the room stood up and applauded.

Amble felt proud. Adele felt proud.

Badger hid again.

She tried to focus again on Mrs Pullalong's strappy shoes. As she did, she decided that these weddings were strange things. But she had to concede, from her place of safety by Mrs Pullalong's toes, they did have some good food!

That chicken in broth was quite her favourite thing.

Chapter 18: Reflections

The special day had come to an end. The newly-weds and Little George had left to go on a honeymoon. All the guests were going home.

As Mrs Poser and Mrs Pullalong got into the taxi, Mrs Pullalong had asked where the happy couple were going for their honeymoon.

Mrs Poser had replied that she didn't know. It was supposed to be a secret. She wasn't sure why. Apparently, it was another of those wedding traditions. Like having a wedding breakfast even though it was well past midday! And for the wedding breakfast to not be toast and marmalade, but a proper sit-down meal.

Amble had wondered what on earth a honeymoon might be. It sounded rather messy. Especially if it was runny honey.

Fortunately, Badger did know.

"It's a holiday for people who have just got married," she explained to Amble. "But I haven't got a clue why it's called a honeymoon."

Amble had to make do with that for the rest of the journey home.

Once they were back, Mrs Poser flopped down on the sofa. She kicked off her shoes and threw the fascinator on to the floor. Amble rested his head on her knees.

It had been an amazing day, and not surprisingly, both Mrs Poser and Amble were now very tired. In fact, Mrs Poser felt too tired to move. She was so glad that Amble had been fed at the wedding breakfast. She didn't think she would be able to budge from her comfortable place, not even to feed him.

Thank goodness she had put out enough food for the cats too.

She could sit down and relax, and think about everything that had happened.

It really had been the most marvellous wedding, and so romantic.

Mrs Poser sighed.

It was hard to believe that such joy could have come from a tragedy.

She remembered how it had all started.

It had all begun with Teaser being killed.

Mrs Poser shuddered as she remembered finding his crumpled body in the bushes. He had looked so small and broken. It was just as well Mrs Pullalong had been with her, or she wouldn't have known what to do!

Then, Mr Helpful had called round with Adele.

Mrs Poser thought she was so incredibly lucky to have

such kind and sympathetic friends. They had taken charge and made sure that Teaser was buried with dignity and kindness, and that she, too, was looked after.

Then, Mr Helpful and Adele had found the kittens. She had gone to see them with the idea of bringing one of them home to help fill the void left by Teaser's death, but when she saw them all together, Mrs Poser had realised that it would be impossible to decide which kitten to have. So, she adopted all three of the little darlings.

Mrs Poser could now tell them apart — but it had been quite tricky at first as they all were very similar to Teaser. Each kitten had his own personality too. Eany was the greedy one. Meany was the hunter of the pack. Mo was the homebody. He could always be found snoozing on Mrs Poser's bed during the day!

Oh, how they made her smile.

It had been quite a risk. Mrs Poser felt that she had been so lucky that both Wafter and Amble had taken to them! She smiled as she remembered how Eany had even fallen asleep in Amble's food bowl.

It was rather strange how most of her thoughts about Amble and the cats seemed to revolve around food!

Mind you, it wasn't just her beloved pets who had a thing about food. Today's wedding breakfast had been simply delicious. But then it had been prepared by the chef who had been Mr Helpful's raffle prize.

Now that raffle prize had been a meal and a half! Even though Mrs Poser had starved herself all day before that slap-up five-course meal, she had still eaten far too much.

And then there was the adventure on the way home. In fact, it was because of that adventure that today had happened.

If Mama Sheep hadn't stood in the middle of the road, the taxi would never have stopped. Mrs Poser and Mrs Pullalong would never have found the little lamb — or perhaps equally importantly — sought help from the RSPCA.

Mrs Poser paused her reflections for a moment so that she could move her leg which was starting to get cramp. Amble's head was quite heavy!

Indeed, if George from the RSPCA (or George Michael as she now knew him to be, she thought with a wry smile) hadn't come out to help, he would never have met the lady from number five (now better known as Dorcas Eliza!)

Although, thinking about it, it was possibly Little George who really helped things along by falling in love with that battered old cat, Feisty Fred.

If Feisty Fred hadn't been adopted, George Michael would never have had a reason to come to number five. And none of today would have happened at all.

Amble was also musing about the day. He particularly remembered the fabulous food — it would be hard not to — those chicken pieces in broth were surely his favourite thing! And how miffed he had been that he hadn't been allowed to lick that magnificent cake.

He certainly had a lot to tell the cats about when they returned from rodent patrol.

He was very impressed that he and Badger had been promoted to be sniffer dogs for the day. That had been such fun. He could run around the room before all the guests arrived and breathe in every glorious smell. At one point, both he and Badger had thought they could smell mice. Had they appeared, the wedding would have been a disaster, but the two dogs had pawed the walls to make sure that any mice knew to keep away.

There were many things about the day that Amble still didn't understand, even though Badger had tried to explain them, but he did understand that George Michael and Dorcas Eliza had made some very serious promises to each other, which meant that George Michael could come and live at number five. Those promises also meant that Little George now had George Michael to help look after him and Feisty Fred. His mother wouldn't have to try and play football any more. Which was probably just as well as she was hopeless at it!

Amble felt sad that the cats couldn't have come today, but he had to agree with Mrs Poser that they weren't good travellers and would have more than likely run off if they had, and then everyone would have had to look for them instead of watching the wedding.

Amble smiled to himself as he remembered how smart Badger and Adele had looked. Their coats were so lovely and shiny.

He also thought that That Other Baby looked very silly in his outfit, although it had to be admitted that it matched the bridesmaids and the bride's dress. Amble didn't understand why everyone had to dress up rather than wear their dog walking clothes and be comfortable, but humans were very strange sometimes.

He shifted his head and settled down at Mrs Poser's feet. Soon, they were both dozing quietly, dreaming of the fun they had had and what a happy day it all had been.

Most definitely their favourite thing!

About the Author

Lynda Thrift lives in the Midlands with her menagerie of cats and dogs. She enjoyed a varied career in pursuit of scientific endeavour, both in the laboratory and in research administration and management. She has now calmed down a little to allow time to walk the dogs, play with the grandchildren and, of course, to write her books.

Ivor Wood, a retired local government lawyer, lives in Coventry with his wife, Ruth and their lovely Labrador who is the role model for Adele, Amble's sister. Ivor and Ruth have had five Guide Dog brood bitches since 1989 and helped raise 131 puppies for the Guide Dogs for the Blind. Karen is their fifth such dog.